Death
of
a
Pew-Potato

THE GUIDE BOOK FOR ALL LAY PEOPLE

This book is layman friendly. No funny Bible words that nobody can pronounce are contained on any pages. Why? IT'S WRITTEN BY A LAYMAN, THAT'S WHY!

Greg Gregoris
Publisher

DEATH OF A PEW - POTATO

FIRST EDITION
Copyright © 1995 by
Greg Gregoris

Scripture quotations marked KJV are from the *King James Version* of the *Bible*, in the public domain.

Verses marked (The Living Bible) are taken from *The Living Bible (c)* 1971. Used by permission of the Tyndale House Publishers, Inc., Wheaton, IL 60189. All rights reserved.

Scripture quotations marked (NIV) are taken from the *Holy Bible, New International Version.* Copyright (c) 1973, 1978, 1984, International Bible Society. Used by permission of Zondervan Bible Publishers. All rights reserved.

Library of Congress Catalog Card Number: 95-95067

ISBN 0-7880-0644-4   PRINTED IN U.S.A.

The Lord God said, "It is not good for the man to be alone. I will make a helper suitable for him. (Gen. 2:18 NIV)

This book is dedicated to the helper God has truly blessed me with.

Tracie, you are the greatest joy that has ever come into my life. I thank the Lord every night for having the opportunity to call you my wife. I could never have written this book without your constant love and your support.

I love you with all my heart.

Greg

Introduction

The Pew-Potato Prayer - Dear Lord, please leave me alone, just let me sit here in my pew on Sunday. And Lord guard my seat, the last seat here in the back row, please don't let anyone else try to sit here. Lord, you know that's my seat. And precious Lord please get me home quickly after the church service on Sunday, before all those church people try an recruit me to actually do something that I don't want to do. Lord make them understand that I'm happy and content just to show up on Sunday. Heavenly Father thank you for hearing my prayer but I've got to go, kick off to the football game is only a minute away. You understand Lord. Thanks God for putting some great games on this week, and thank you for that all sports cable channel. See you next Sunday Lord. Amen.

****

An individual in our church made a comment that really caught my attention and got me to thinking. He said you can't judge the success of a church by how many people show up on Sunday. That's funny, I thought the only way you could judge a church was by their Sunday attendance. Didn't you? He continued by saying the way to judge the success of the church is by what is happening in the church Monday through Saturday. I just always assumed the church was closed during these days. The gentleman continued to make his point by saying that the one hour worship service on Sunday is important, but it can't stop there. The Sunday worship service is the easy part of being a Christian. He claimed that the real work of the church is done after the Sunday service, and it's being done by people who are not afraid to get **involved** in their faith and in their church. I didn't want to hear this kind of message, even though I knew it was true. Why didn't I want to hear this message? Because I was a professional pew-potato and this message went against my creed (see above prayer). I just wanted to put in my hour in the pew every Sunday and head home, not to be seen or heard from until next Sunday. Plus I had to get home to catch the Sunday sports shows. I love watching them all, and for some reason the best games are always on Sunday. I have to be home watching the games, that's what makes me happy. God wants me to be happy, doesn't He?

God does want me to be happy, but He was about to show me a happiness that I didn't believe was possible. He set out to teach me real happiness through **involvement** with my church. To my surprise the church is open Monday through Saturday. Here's the weird part, people actually show up on these "off" days. So what are these people doing in the church on these "off" days? Glad you asked. That's what this book is all about. It's about the great work that God is doing through His churches, and how the Sunday message actually gets carried out during the other six days. The only problem is only a few people (20%)are **involved** in this worthy and rewarding effort. Their efforts are truly being blessed by God, and don't we all want God's blessing? I know I do. So I guess I better start to learn about this church **involvement** thing that seems to please God so much.

This is my story on how God took me, the all-star pew-potato, and got me showing up at the church on those "off" days. And to my complete amazement, God has showed me how much enjoyment this work can be. I was very leery at first, but now I'm completely sold on this beautiful concept of **"involvement."** God has "peeled" this pew-potato and has shown me the true meaning of His joy. A joy that I didn't think was possible by just getting **involved** in those stupid church projects (that's what I use to call them). I don't call them stupid anymore, because I have witnessed what God can do through the smallest of church projects. He can change a human beings life, in other words He can perform miracles even in the smallest of tasks.

This book was written for people who are hesitant or afraid to say "yes" for whatever reasons to a church project, and for those people who like me (pew-potato) saw no reason to get **involved**. Let this book give you the encouragement and opportunity to experience the exciting adventure that God will place upon you for helping the church, His church, His house.

Jesus said; And on this rock I will build my church, and the gates of Hades will not overcome it (Matt. 16:18 NIV).

Greg Gregoris

CONTENTS

Chapter One

"Pew-Potato Fever"

I wanted to be a pew-potato, which very much parallels a couch-potato (sit and do nothing), but God wouldn't let me. For some reason God had a plan for me in the church and wouldn't let me get comfortable just vegetating for one hour in a pew every Sunday and telling people I was extremely religious because I never missed church. No, God had a different plan and that's how this layman's story begins.

They say most men fear the "C" word (commitment) when it comes to love and relationships. At least that's what every woman in my life has indicated to me to be true. I'm sure there is some truth to this, but I have discovered something even more consistent then that in both male and female behavior. That is to absolutely fear this one particular activity that could without a doubt destroy the way most everybody is enjoying their religious experience. I call this the "I" word syndrome, with the "I" standing for **INVOLVEMENT**.

I thought I was pretty clear in my oral contract with God that if He would just leave me alone I would in return guarantee Him a regular attendance come every Sunday. Except of course while I was on vacation. Nobody is expected to go to church while on vacation - right! I'm pretty sure this vacation exclusion concept is stated somewhere in Proverbs.

Little did I know and without any warning God was about to make dramatic changes in this layman's attitude towards my role in the church. I always assumed my role in the church to be two fold. One, was to be there every Sunday and sit in the same pew seat (God place a plague upon anyone who dares sit in MY PEW SEAT). Second, was to give God a few bucks in the collection plate each week. Again, except on vacation. Even God knows you need some extra money while your on vacation. I'm sure this vacation thing is stated in Proverbs or maybe it's in one of King David's Psalms, he liked to travel.

My personal view of the church, and I certainly felt it was the only correct view, was that the pastor gets paid the big bucks to run "everything" in the church, why should I step in and mess things up. Wouldn't that make God mad? I mean let's face it, don't all pastors go to those fancy religious schools with big crosses on them. I have to assume once they get out of those religious schools they must know everything about God and His church. Wouldn't you agree? So why should I, with a public school education and a B.A. in business from a small college with no crosses on it go into partnership with these powerful God knowing, Bible carrying servants of the Lord. What could I possibly have in common with a pastor to make this partnership work? I'm sure the pastor would even find something wrong with the ordinary things us pew-potatoes do, like cheat a little in golf. I just know the pastor will say that's wrong, so how could we ever get along on a church project? Impossible - right!

Well, it turns out I was wrong. Except about the cheating in golf part, darn it! It turns out the pastor has the same human frailties that I do. I never considered this before. My initial reaction to this astonishing news was to tell my pastor he should file a lawsuit against the school for leaving in the human frailties part. I also discovered he didn't learn "everything" about God in those fancy religious schools with the big crosses on them. And I even found out on my own something more startling, that God often speaks to me directly without even asking for permission from my pastor. That God can be a sneaky fellow when He wants to. As a matter of fact God has told me a lot of things about life that He hasn't bothered sharing with the pastor. Even a self-desiring pew-potato like me was able to come to these two conclusions;

1. God is probably talking to other people in the church without seeking the pastor's permission, and

2. In certain situations that come up in the life of a church, the lay people are the best equipped to deal with it.

After mediating for about 5 seconds on the above conclusions, God made it perfectly clear that the pastor desperately needs the laymen's **involvement** to run a church the way God intended. OH WELL, THERE GOES MY PEW-POTATO STATUS.

My next emotional response was, but why me God, WHY ME? I just wanted to go to church on Sunday and make the church pews look full, and who knows maybe even learn something while I'm there. I got to believe that a full church pleases you, right Lord? I'm even willing to throw $5 or perhaps $10 dollars in the collection plate, that is if I have any money left by Sunday after paying the bills. Got to pay the bills, plus Friday and Saturday nights are good nights to go out have fun and I just know your unconditional love means for me to have fun. Isn't that right Lord? I mean you already have to be proud of me. I know by heart both the Lord's Prayer and the Apostles' Creed. That alone has to put me on your "most favorite" list. I know probably everybody knows the Lord's Prayer but what about the Apostles' Creed? I learned it in Junior High and have never forgotten it, so I have to be ranked ahead of those other faithful pew-potato Christians. Go pick on the people who don't know the Apostles' Creed and give me back my comfortable church lifestyle of visiting your house once a week for one hour. Let's be honest, nobody wants guests hanging around their house for hours - right!

Wrong Greg! Apparently God actually likes visitors to hang around (go figure). God always seems to be doing things different than most of us. God has also told me that He thinks it's nice, but that He is not overly impressed that I know the Apostles' Creed by heart. **WHAT!** Not overly impressed that I know the Apostles' Creed, what does this guy want from me? Then He told me. Greg, I want the "I" word syndrome from you. I want your **involvement**. It had come to this, my happy, peaceful, hands-off layman's lifestyle was going to change forever. Christ was about to slowly nudge me into the arena of **involvement**.

It was at this point in my so-called religious life that Christ made me realize that great churches are not just developed or created by great pastors. They're created by pastors and

13

lay people working together getting **involved** and jointly doing great things for God's Kingdom here on earth.

Help your pastors, they truly do need you and that's a fact. Apparently those fancy religious schools with big crosses on them leave things out on purpose. How else could your pastor grow, but more importantly how else could you grow.

It was only a year ago that if you asked me how a church should go about growing, I would have told you to hire a dynamic pastor and have him hit the community streets to influence people to come to his church. Isn't that what we pay a pastor to do? Shouldn't that be one of his jobs in the church? I mean doesn't he just hang around the church all day anyway, why not put him to some good use like soliciting those rotten church avoiding heathens who live right next door to me. I keep wondering when the pastor will get around to visiting these people. It's long overdue.

Once again, God gave me an answer I kind of didn't want to hear and I certainly was surprised by it. It definitely isn't the way I would have handled the situation. God said the pastor is not going to visit those rotten church avoiding heathen neighbors of mine. Well God, then who is? God said I've decided to send you. **WHAT**! Lord you must be losing your mind. Don't you remember I went to a college with no crosses on the buildings. I have no training, what could I possibly teach my church avoiding heathen neighbors on the subject of God? God said, how about the Apostles' Creed, you are always reminding people that you know by heart. Start with that. And there was the simple answer for me. Start with something you do know well, and then God will take it from there. There is no doubt in my mind that the Nike Company must of plagiarized God when they came out with the slogan "Just Do It."

Take it from me, the all-star pew potato, don't be afraid to step forward the next time your church needs something accomplished. You could be the very person God has called to fill that need in His church. And don't worry about talent and experience. God will take care of that for you. Maybe that's why God has now placed this book in your hands. God has a tremendous track record of doing some amazing things through people who felt they were under qualified for the job. Need proof? How about Moses, Gideon and Jonah to name a few. All three men wanted God to leave them alone, and that evidence is clearly stated right in the Bible. Moses said; But who am I, that I should go to Pharaoh and bring the Israelites out of Egypt (Exodus 3:11 NIV). Gideon said: But Lord how can I save Israel? My clan is the weakest in Manasseh and I am the least of my family (Judges 6:15 NIV). Jonah easily tops both Moses and Gideon, he skips out of town on a boat (Jonah 1:3, more about Jonah in the next chapter).

All three of these men in their own way acted like a modern day pew-potato and begged God not to use them, claiming that someone else is more equipped to handle the responsibility that God was trying to give to them. These great men of the Bible, Moses, Gideon, and Jonah were all reluctant in the beginning, but all three ended up performing miracles for the glory of God. Praise the Lord that He was persistent in getting these three men **involved** in His work. I ask that you take that leap to get **involved**, because God's resume shows that He has taken reluctant pew-potatoes in the past and has performed incredible blessings to both the individual and His Kingdom here on earth.

Chapter Two

Jonah: "The Pew-Potato's Hero"

How can you possibly call yourself a pew-potato and not love this Bible guy Jonah. He was everything a pew-potato aspires to be. What a role model for us. Jonah even makes me feel obedient and I wasn't sure that was possible. He shows all the character traits of what pew-potatoes hope to achieve, or make that not to achieve in our commitment to the church.

Jonah certainly thought he was the wrong person for the job God was trying to give him. And let's be honest my fellow pew-potatoes, don't we feel the same way when someone asks us to perform a certain function for the church. Don't we want to give Jonah's answer of thank you very much but I'm just not the right guy for the job. Hey, I like that, now that's a smooth answer. It sounds honest and you are even admitting that you have some faults (nice touch). God would have to be pleased with this, you are being honest, right? I mean why would God want to put some-body unqualified on an important job? My own common sense and the business education I received from that small college with no crosses on it taught me that this would be a disaster.

Well it seems that God didn't go to the same college I did, because He stuck to His choice of using this unqualified Jonah. When reading about Jonah my pew-potato heart just goes right out to him, and I want to yell up to God to just cut Jonah some slack. Get off the guy's back. You're asking too much from him. God was lucky there weren't any Labor Unions back in those days because He certainly seems to be involved in unfair bargaining negotiations. How would you like to negotiate your next contract from inside a fish. To me that seems like a real drawback.

I now had to ask myself something, where were the lawyers

back in those days. Why couldn't an aggressive attorney represent Jonah and tell God to stop harassing his client or he would place a restraining order on Him. Have this attorney set God straight. You just can't go around throwing people inside whales. There's got to be a law against that. Let's face it God, Jonah's not interested in your latest offer, so leave him alone. Don't you understand God, that Jonah's job is to inspire pew-potatoes like Greg Gregoris to politely turn down all that stupid extra curriculum stuff that the church thinks is so important. By the way, it's not that us pew-potatoes don't want to help, it's just we don't have the time. This is especially true during football season.

I have to grudgingly give God credit here. One trait I do admire is persistence and God is certainly persistent with Jonah. Apparently Jonah was so sure of God's persistence that he runs away right from the beginning. Well, make that floats away since he took a boat. I felt after reading this part in the Bible that God must really be "digging" me now. Yes, I freely admit to being a pew-potato and wanting to be left alone, but I never ran away..... or did I?

Church going pew-potatoes have developed the incredible skill of running away without ever moving. How do I know this, because I have done these things. Whenever someone at my church or the pastor has a special announcement to make like needing people to help paint the church, it's amazing how fast I can grab one of the Hymnals and bury my face into it and actually look like I'm being profoundly touched by the words on the page. You can't expect me to show up and paint if I missed the announcement. That makes sense doesn't it? And remember it wasn't my fault I missed the announcement, I was just getting prepared to sing praises to the Lord. Yeah Right!

My all time favorite maneuver is what I like to call the "great escape." The great escape calls for timing and speed. I even taught my wife this trick. What you do is as soon as the church service ends you bolt and I do mean bolt for the door. It's a real plus if you can beat the pastor to the door before he starts his greetings. And if you're real fortunate the church will have side doors you can race to, so you can totally avoid greeting anyone. You won't make many friends this way but most pew-potatoes have enough outside friends anyway. At least that's what I thought. Who needs church friends, isn't their role to trick you into doing something you don't want to do. They can't trick you into doing something if by the time they are getting out of their pews you are already in the church parking lot racing for the car and heading home. Who wants to be bothered with that fellowship baloney anyway. I was there for the important stuff like the singing and listening to the sermon. What more could possibly be asked of me. Wouldn't you agree?

Well after reading what I just wrote it looks like Jonah and I do have a similar problem after all, doesn't it? My running away is just not as obvious as Jonah's. I mean I'm not getting on a boat and sailing to a different country, but I was ducking all responsibilities or callings the Lord could have been asking me to help out with. I just thought that every church had a certain group of people who enjoyed doing all the work in the church. You mean I could be wrong again? It does seem pretty clear that our pew-potato hero Jonah got into worse trouble by running away. Wow, it looks like none of my inactive theories are going to hold water. Sorry about that Jonah.

Jonah displays another popular attitude of the pew-potato when finally convinced to get into action. That is, well I'll do it, but you can't make me like it (Jonah 4:1-3). There's no way I will fully throw myself into this project. If I do it reluctantly, the church won't bother me again. I'll show them. I have since learned one major flaw in this theory of reluctant performance. You see it is not the church that is asking you to get into action, it's God Himself. And no tasks are considered too small or insignificant in God's eyes. They're all important to Him.

I had a hard time understanding why small things that probably anyone could do would be so pleasing to someone like Almighty God. Doesn't the name Almighty God mean He wants big things being done? Well, yes and no. Some people will do big things for God, but here's the weird part. God is just as pleased with those people who do little things for Him. Once again I must point out that God is not acting rational.....or is He.

19

The first assignment I got stuck with, I mean that I supposedly volunteered for was cleaning the church. Exciting way to get **involved** with the church, wouldn't you agree? This certainly validated my four year college degree. Let's be honest you don't have to be in your second year of college to know how to plug in a vacuum cleaner. And now here comes the bonus part, for doing a good job of vacuuming the church, I then got the opportunity to dust it. Wow, was I putting my degree to good use or what? But it didn't stop there. Oh no! Apparently once you pass the church dusting exam they promote you to the final detail of church cleaning. And what glorious duty is that you might ask? It was now my job to clean the church bathrooms. Hallelujah, Greg has hit the big time.

My pew-potato instincts starting coming back to me when I was driving home from the first time I helped clean the church. Things like I don't even clean up my own mess most of the time, why am I now cleaning other people's messes. It was at this time God decided to lend me a hand in coming up with the right answer.

God reminded me that one of the things I like best about my church, even in the pew-potato status, was how clean it was every Sunday. For some reason I just assumed that churches were like those new self-cleaning ovens. Once everybody was out of the church God would open the windows and blow everything out into the street. Once in the streets the local municipal cleaning teams could take it from there. That's what we pay taxes for, right! To keep our streets clean. God was just using the system the way it was suppose to be used and creating jobs at the same time.

Well, I got some bad employment news for the people on those local municipal cleaning teams. It seems God doesn't clean His church that way. His method is to use the people who attend the church to clean it for Him. This realization brought two emotions upon me. One was gratitude. I took for granted and didn't bother to understand that people just like me were keeping my church spotless, and providing me with a great environment to worship. Today, I truly am thankful for the people who get **involved** and keep God's house clean. I now understand how important this is to God. This might have seemed small to me at one time, but it's never small to God. Nothing we do ever is. My second emotion was one of anger. Since God is not blowing everything out into the streets, why are my local taxes so high.

My **involvement** in the church has grown since my exposure to the cleaning team, but my wife and I are still on the cleaning team and we're proud to be a part of it. I look at it this way, what would impress a new visitor to our church? If your answer is stained glass windows, I agree with you, but our church doesn't have any. Since we don't have the stained glass windows, how about a clean church? There is no doubt in my mind that a clean church would at least subconsciously impress a new visitor. And who can tell, maybe that new visitor could someday be the most **involved** member of our entire congregation, doing great things for God. So do I personally think that the Lord is pleased when lay people do something as minor as clean the church? YOU BET I DO.

So who knows maybe God is asking you to get **involved** in your church by picking up a toilet brush. Don't laugh, that's how He started me out. Am I embarrassed about starting out this way? Not at all. I'll pick up a toilet brush for God any day of the week.

Chapter Three

Can A Pew-Potato Say "NO"
(Without God Turning You Into A Pillar Of Salt)

There is an interesting phenomenon that takes place once the pew-potato gives his first "yes" to a church project. Apparently the next logical step for all churches to take is to request your time and service on every committee the church has. I believe it's some kind of Bible law the church has to strictly adhere to. They won't tell me where it's at in the Bible, but I have a sneaky feeling it might be in that 1st Chronicles book.

The only other layman's answer I can come up with is there must have been amendments added on to the Ten Commandments about church **involvement**, but only pastors and committee chair people know about it. I have noticed in church recently that some people have a bigger Bible than I do. The pastor's Bible is certainly bigger than mine. GOOD LORD THAT'S IT! That church **involvement** amendment must only be in those big Bibles. I have got to get me one of those big Bibles.

My first reaction to combat this church **involvement** amendment was to call my attorney friend and ask if it was legal for a layman to have his phone number changed to an unlisted number. My attorney friend asked if I was a Protestant or a Catholic? I said what difference does that make? He said probably none, but since he was charging me a consultation fee he wanted to make it look like he had done some research. He explained to me that an attorney can charge a higher fee when research is involved. So what's the answer I asked? He said he hadn't done enough research yet. At this particular moment, he admitted he wasn't sure. He said he would get back in touch with me later, and then verified my mailing address so he knew where to send my invoice. Did I mention he was my friend. So I was on my own to see if I could set the record for church **involvement** in one week.

Why was I so afraid to say no to the church in the beginning? I'll tell why in one word, GUILT. I was afraid people would get mad at me if I said no. Worst yet, God would get mad at me if I said no. And we all know what happens when God gets mad at you, don't we? He turns you into a pillar of salt. That Bible guy named Lot can verify this truth. I don't want to be a pillar of salt, do you? And besides, salt's not even good for you anymore. There's only one way out now, just say yes to everything. Become the "yes man" and then everybody will love me, right! By the way, I believe that God is a very current and up with the times God. He would not turn you into a pillar of salt. I think it would be a pillar of Sweet'N Low.

So the question still remains, how can I say no to certain things and not feel guilty about it? Try this one on for size. Because it's Biblical to say no. Look at all the examples the Bible gives us about how God answers prayers. God certainly answers all prayers. He either says yes, not yet, or NO! That's right, God says no, and if that answer is good enough for Him, it certainly is good enough for you and me.

I believe that God says no to some of our prayer requests because He knows that request is just not right for us. Well the same principal applies when the church asks a request that you know is not right for you. Turn it down, say no. But won't the church people be mad at me now for saying no? I doubt it, that's not the nature of a true Christian. You see Christians are reminded that Jesus in the Garden of Gethsemane (Matt. 26:39) asked God if it was possible to take away from Him this cup of death. God did answer His son's request, He said no.

Did Jesus get mad at His Father? Once again the answer is no. Jesus still loved God. And the church people will still love you, even when you say no. And if for some reason they do get mad, don't worry about it. They have the problem, not you. I seriously doubt any church person would get mad though. How do I know this? Because at one time they were in your shoes. You see we were all pew-potatoes at one time in our lives.

24

Here's three suggestions I would like to pass along to my fellow pew-potatoes who have recently said yes to their first church **involvement**, or are thinking about saying yes in the near future.

1. Never make an immediate decision on the spot. Don't say yes or no. The only way that you can truly know if God has chosen you for this responsibility is to ask Him. Tell the person you want to pray about it and you will get back to them.

2. Pray about it. Ask God to help make this decision clear to you. If you are the right person for the job God will tell you. God will also tell you if you're not the right person. But never give an answer until you prayerfully considered it.

3. Call back the person with the answer God has given you. How could anyone possibly get mad at you when all you are doing is relaying God's answer.

Is it possible to get too **involved** with the church? No Way! That's got to be impossible - right? I mean after all, this is God's house. Shouldn't I be here 23 1/2 hours a day, seven days a week?

I guess it's okay to be at the church 23 1/2 hours a day, seven days a week, if you are still single and the pastor of a church. And if you have absolutely no knowledge of any living family members. Personally I don't know anyone who matches this description. But if I ever meet someone who does, I will do my duty and direct them to the nearest church.

So my layman's answer to the question can you get too **involved** with the church, is yes, most definitely. If your church **involvement** starts taking you away from spending quality time with your family, "knock it off". Cut back, stay at home more often. I personally can't think of anything more important to God than the family unit.

I know the intentions are good when on a Wednesday night you miss your son's Little League game because you're at the church working late on a special project that you feel obligated to. But my common sense layman's diagnosis of this situation is that you have not prayed enough to the Lord about your role in the church. I know I didn't attend one of those fancy religious schools with crosses on them, but I do feel this in my heart, "layman heart to layman heart", so to speak. That if you asked the Lord what is my priority, to be at the church or at my son's Little League game? I firmly believe the Lord would toss you a catcher's mitt and say see you at the game.

I can hear every pew-potato baseball fan cheering now. Hey, Greg said that during baseball season I can avoid the church, and he feels the Lord told him to say it. I can certainly live under those rules. Now, who do I need to speak with to get me out of church during football, soccer, and basketball seasons. You see if you give a pew-potato an inch, they'll take a mile. Remember, I practiced very hard to be the best pew-potato I could be. And I just loved escape clauses when it came to avoiding church work.

In my best season as a pew-potato I would have loved this Little League escape clause. I would've tried to convince the pastor and the church leadership that my son has Little League games every night. That's right, every night from April til October. They're going to play all their regularly scheduled games plus make up all the rained out games for the last ten years. I'm sure the church would totally support the decision I made to closely follow my son's activities, right? Talk to me in November, I might be ready to get **involved** then. Of course we all know that youth basketball and in-door soccer starts in November (I told you I was a good pew-potato).

So how does a pew-potato who has finally said yes to the church keep his life in balance? First of all, balance is the key word. Up to this point the pew-potato has to realize it's been 100% outside **involvement**, and 0% church **involvement**. There is no balance so far. But it is just as important to make sure the balance doesn't tilt completely the other way, 100% church **involvement** and 0% outside **involvement**. There has to be a checks and balance system set up.

So what's the answer for the pew-potato when concerned with time **involvement** for the church. Do I say yes, or do I say no? Here's the answer the Lord gave me, the all-star pew potato. You say both, but first ask God what He thinks is right for you. He will always direct you to the right answer. Why am I so sure God will give you the right answer every time? Because He loves us unconditionally and He promises to help us always. I can't say it with any more elegance than how it's already written in the Bible in that one beautiful passage in Isaiah; For I am the Lord, your God, who takes hold of your right hand and says to you, Do not fear; I will help you (Isaiah 41:13 NIV). Wow, what a great checks and balance system.

Chapter Four

Who's In Charge Here?

Numbers and statistics have always fascinated me. You see there is real power in numbers. One rule known as Pareto's Law or the 20/80 rule states that 20% of the people in your organization will do 80% of the work. This rule certainly applies to most congregations. Sometimes it seems more like the 10/90 rule. But here's the weird part. Follow me on this one. If only 20% of your congregation is **involved** in your church's activities, that means 80% are pew-potatoes. Wait it gets weirder. Remember I said that there is power in numbers. Just look at the election process in our country. Who always wins? The party with the highest percent of the votes, right? If your church took a congregational vote today what group of people would control the highest percent of votes in your church? It's those pew-potatoes. So who's in charge of the church? Apparently it's those pew-potatoes.

Now pastors, try to stay calm. You have one great historical mystery that's working on your side. Though the pew-potatoes are in control, they don't know it and probably never will. So go ahead pastors, go back to bed and get a good night's sleep.

I know during my pew-potatoes days I had no clue I had this much power. Too bad, maybe I could have passed some of my favorite "inactive theories" when I was in a position of power. I know I would have canceled all Sunday evening meetings or services during the fall. Why? Because ESPN now shows football games on Sunday nights. Isn't that great, three football games every Sunday. Do we live in a great country or what!

I finally had the guts to ask myself, what would my pew-potato church look like if I had decided to enforce my pew-potato majority status?

Well, it would look like this:

• Shorter Sermons - Boy, those pastors love to hear themselves talk. They must think that's why we're there, to listen to them. Will somebody volunteer to bring them into the real world. I only come so that God will bless me with my good attendance mark. We all know that's how you get to heaven, by how many times you went to church on Sunday. Here I am God, mark me present. Bye-Bye God, I'll see you next Sunday.

• ATM Machines In The Church Narthex - The church is always bugging me for my money. So why don't they make it a little easier for me to get to it so I can give them some. And why not accept Visa/MC, it's the American way to go into debt via the credit card. Let us pew-potatoes charge our monthly tithes, I'll bet there would be an increase. Boy, these church people are sure behind the times.

• Drive Thru Window For Communion - All pew-potatoes dislike Communion Sunday. The service now lasts 1 1/2 hours, and during the fall that definitely cuts into the NFL Pre-Game Show. Pew-potatoes always sit in the back of the church (for quick escapes, we already covered this) so we are the last to get served the Communion elements. Now seriously think about this time saving concept of a drive thru. You drive up get your piece of bread and your grape juice, say Amen, and be on your way (don't want to hold up the people behind you). All other places that serve food have a drive thru. McDonalds has a drive thru. Burger King and Wendy's both have a drive thru. Even my hometown Pizza Hut has a drive thru. Once again the church is behind the times. When will they learn to modernize. This drive thru Communion idea would cut 40 minutes out of the service. Come on people get with it, us pew-potatoes want to get home.

• The Pastoral Prayer Has Got To Go - Only two people really enjoy this part of the service. One of course is the pastor, the other is the local Chiropractor because of all the bad necks from having your head bowed for 20 minutes. Why does the pastor feel it's necessary to individually name every sick person on the planet and tell us what their ailments are? Doesn't God know these people are sick? Of course He does. So why doesn't the pastor just say,

Dear God you know who's sick, heal a bunch of them, Amen. That sounds like a pretty good prayer to me. If he would only start doing this I know I could now make that NFL Pre-Game Show. When will those men of the cloth learn to pray like us layman? Soon I hope. I'm starting to have a sneaky feeling that pastors are paid by the hour. And we all know that when you work on Sundays and holidays that's double time by good union standards.

• Let's Just Sit - Why all the standing and then sitting? What's going on here? What is it, do we sit, or do we stand? Make up your minds. Why all this up and down, and up and down stuff? If I wanted a physical workout I would have stayed at home and put in my Jane Fonda aerobic tape. Just let everybody relax, take a load off and sit through the Service. Hey, we need to sit, we all had a tough week, wouldn't you agree? And you mean to tell me the only way God can hear us sing is if we are standing, who started this rumor? It must be one of those funny church laws that's only in those big Bibles that I spoke about earlier. I just got to get me one of those big Bibles.

So let's sum up my pew-potato church service. Well, we all get to sit, and we're out in 20 minutes. Broadcast this type of church service in your neighborhood and your church will be overflowing every Sunday. People from other states would want to come to your church services if this is what you were offering. But why? Because the majority rules and the pew-potatoes are in the majority everywhere in the U.S. Since pew-potatoes make up 80% of most churches, I think it's safe to assume that they, or people who think like them, make up 80% of our total population. "Pew-Potato Fever - Catch It If You Can."

I think this proves without a shadow of a doubt that there is real power in numbers, and that the pew-potatoes must have all the power.....or do they?

I didn't come to realize I had any power until I decided to switch sides over to the minority party (the 20% group) and get **involved**. Once again I feel it's my duty to point out that God is not acting rational. We all know the majority rules, that's what democracy is all about. It's the foundation of our great nation. It seems this majority rule concept has been "vetoed" by God when it comes to His church. Then who's in charge of running the church? Are you ready for this answer, you might want to sit down when I tell you this. It's the minority. WHAT! Let me see if I got this right. The little skimpy 20% minority is calling all the shots in the church? That's right. Hey, wait a minute, does the other 80% of the people know about this? We tried to tell them, but they said they didn't want to get **involved**.

God once again is acting in reverse of what I had learned in college. I'm starting to think that the college I went to did a bad job. I was taught when you build something you must get as many people **involved** as you can, and 80% certainly seems larger to me than 20%. So you go out to the 80% people (the majority) and empower them and let them take ownership of it, and then you build something really great. That sounds right, doesn't it? Come on God get with the program. Answer me this God, why is it that you would choose the little skimpy 20% to build and run your church? That just doesn't make any sense. Explain this to me Lord. And then He did!

Apparently God always chooses the little guy to do His big work. How about David and Goliath. If you were there, and let's be completely honest, who would you have bet on? Did you ever wonder why God just didn't go out and get a bigger dude than Goliath to go kick his butt. I think the real answer is given to us by Paul in 2nd Corinthians. Paul makes a strange comment, he says that power is made perfect in weakness. He continues by saying therefore, when I am weak, then I am strong (2 Cor. 12:9-10). Do you want to confuse us pew-potatoes. Throw that line at us a couple of times. When you are weak, then you are strong. What's that all about?

God finally busted through my thick skull and showed me this concept at work right here in my own church. Here's how my conversation with God went:

God: Who has all the power in your church?
Greg: The 80%, they're in the majority.
God: Wrong!
God: Who did my servant Paul in Scriptures say had the power?
Greg: I believe he said the weak skimpy people, or something like that.

32

God: Correct! Well, close enough.

God: Who do you consider to be in a position of weakness at your church?

Greg: That's simple, the skimpy 20%, they're in the minority.

God: Correct! Good answer.

God: Now Greg, back to my first question. Based upon Scripture who have I given the power to in your church?

Greg: The weak people Lord. The little skimpy 20% who are in the minority. They are actually the strong ones.

God: You finally got it correct my child. And Greg, don't take this personally, but your ideas about the pew-potato church service. I think they stink.

Greg: ME TOO!

Chapter Five

Oh Honey, I Signed Us Up For Bible Study Or We Just Joined A Cult!

Bible Study was actually the first activity my wife Tracie and I got involved with in the church. I always list the cleaning team first because for some unknown reason I consider Bible Study an outside the church activity. In my way of thinking if you don't have to drive to the church, it's an outside activity. Plus, I was always afraid to tell my secular friends I was going to Bible Study (they might laugh and call me a religious nut). So how did I handle it when my secular friends would ask me where I was going on Wednesday nights? I felt I did what the majority of first time nervous and insecure Bible Study people would have done. I LIED! I told them I was going to meetings, knowing that they would think I meant business meetings. I was off to a great start, wouldn't you agree?

I accepted the invitation to attend Bible Study for one reason. I didn't have the guts to say no, and because I liked the gentleman who asked me. In my defense, I was curious about this thing called Bible Study. It did intrigue me. So when I informed my wife that I had signed us up for Bible Study, she asked a very good question. What do you do at a Bible Study? I had never thought about that before. I had to be honest with her, I wasn't sure. I think we go over to somebody's house and pray on their front lawn. She didn't think that was right.

My wife wanted to know more about this Bible Study group I had committed us to. Things like, who's in it? I didn't know, I only knew the one person who had asked me to join and that was it. It was at this moment a horrible thought crossed my mind. Maybe I didn't join a Bible Study, but instead signed us up with one of those wacko religious cults. Great, that means next year at this time I'll be at the airport with my head shaved passing out literature that the world is coming to an end. Boy, why did I say yes so easily. What happened to that let me pray about it line? Why didn't I use it?

Well, it turns out we didn't join a wacko religious cult (too bad, I do like the airport). Bible Study actually turned out to be a great decision. My wife and I got to meet new people in the church and we started learning a lot. But there was a lot of anxiety in the beginning, at least for me there was. My wife always handles things better than I do.

First of all my wife and I were replacing another couple that had left this Bible Study. Who was the other couple? Only the church pastor and his wife. I felt I was in trouble right away. I knew my wife was okay, that she could match up pretty well against the pastor's wife, but what about me? Think about the trade off here. This Bible Study group was losing its pastor, its leader and the most knowledgeable person in the whole group about this subject matter. And what were they getting in return? A guy who thought Bible Study was when you pray on someone's front lawn! Now you know why I was so nervous in the beginning.

The next fear that came over me was when I found out this group I was joining had already been together for three whole years. Wow, it sure is taking this group a long time to read the Bible. I got my college degree in four years. These people must be reading the Bible at a clip of one word per week.

Of course my most obvious fear was, what if they ask me to read. Especially that Old Testament stuff. I can't pronounce any of those funny Bible names. They'll all laugh at me. By the way, why would any parent of any generation name their child Amaziah or Jehoshaphat? What was wrong with these people? Didn't they know they were making history and that someday I would have to pronounce their names in Bible Study. When God calls me home to heaven, I'm going to have a long talk with these people about some of their ridiculous names. I wonder why nobody named Bob, Ed or Deb were doing great things back then. Oh well, enough whining.

I did discover something interesting in my Bible Study. The other people in my group who had three years experience on me in Bible Study, butchered those funny names as bad as I did. I'm even starting to wonder if the pastor is pronouncing these names correctly. How do we really know he is pronouncing it correctly? Think about that for a moment. I'm thinking the pastor is getting a free ride on these names because we all just assume that he's pronouncing it correctly because he went to one of those schools with crosses on the buildings. I'll have to ask the pastor about this.

We do something interesting in our Bible Study with those hard to pronounce Bible names, and it's working out quite well for us. Here's our new attack plan to these names. However the reader pronounces the name (right or wrong, it doesn't matter), that's what we will call him all night. Simple enough isn't it? One night one of us was reading a chapter in the Gospel of Luke (it wasn't me) and they came to this individual's name, Judas Iscariot. Well our reader looked at it and then proceeded to pronounce it like this; Judas Is A Carrot. So that's what we called him all night, Judas Is A Carrot. Bible Study is allowed to be fun you know!

My first Bible Study crisis developed when our group decided to split into two groups. More people from our church wanted to join these small groups so it was felt we needed more groups meeting on different nights so that everybody could participate. Here's when the problem came into play. Our leader decided to volunteer to go to another group. Our group now did not have a leader and so it was decided that we would rotate the leadership role. WHAT! What do you mean rotate the leadership role? I have to lead a Bible Study one week? Are you guys nuts! I don't know the Bible, I've only been in the group for a couple of weeks. The only Bible verse I know by heart is John 3:16; For God so loved the world, He gave us the bright Sun.

I started having tremendous pew-potato attacks. I wanted to yell, please just leave me alone. I know, maybe I'll tell them I got a new night job, or that somebody stole my Bible. Hey, I like that one, I'll say that a Christian burglar broke into my house and stole all my Bibles. You can't lead a Bible Study without a Bible, right? Well, my group was prepared for this, apparently they had extra Bibles that they were glad to lend me. Rats! I should have known this was going to happen. Christians are always trying to give you something. It's better to give than to receive, and my group was living up to this by supplying me with Bibles.

They gave me Bibles I have never heard of before. One was the Life Application Bible (I own one of these now), and the other was the Serendipity Bible to help me prepare questions for our Bible lesson when it was my turn to lead the group. The plot thickens...

We were studying the book of Ephesians when it was my turn to be leader and guess what chapter I got to lead. Chapter 5, something about women being submissive to men. Thanks for starting me out with such an easy lesson Lord. Half our group is female, they're going to hate me. My wife is going to hate me, probably my mother and sister will hate me after this lesson. Dear God, are you sure I'm the one you want leading this lesson? I suppose next week you'll assign me Revelations so I can tell the group the whole world is coming to an end. I'm basically a nice guy, and I love and respect women. I just want to be liked. How can I get out of leading this lesson? I couldn't! Read on...

It turns out all my worries about this chapter were needless. None of the women in my group were offended by what the word of God was saying to them. Just the opposite. They actually found it a blessing to be hearing this message and found great joy in trying to be obedient to it. Calling all single guys out there. Do you want to meet the perfect woman, the girl of your dreams? Someone who will make you happy and love you with all her heart. Someone who will make you feel special and loved. Well, I've got some news for you bachelors out there. These wonderful women do exist, but you won't find them at any single's bar. They're hanging out in your local churches Bible Study groups. Go check it out.

I learned two interesting things in leading our group through Ephesians Chapter 5. First, I learned that you never let a man read verse 22 because he'll stop and shout "Amen" at the end of that verse. At least that's what our reader did. We use the New International Version (NIV) Bible in our group and verse 22 was read like this by our exhilarated male reader; Wives, (he then stared straight at his wife) submit to your husbands as to the Lord. He then stood up shouted "Amen", and then closed his Bible while declaring the Bible Study to be over based on the grounds there was nothing more important to learn, God had spoken. So it's important to remember if you ever lead a group in Ephesians Chapter 5, only allow the females to read verses 22-24.

The second interesting thing I learned while preparing this lesson, was that it's really the men who have the bigger commitment here. Now don't get mad at me you beautiful Christian ladies, but according to Ephesians 5:25 us men folk are suppose to give up our lives for you. Christ gave His life for the church and apparently He expects the same from us men. Now I completely understand why my friend stopped after verse 22.

I now have lead our Bible Study group quite frequently, and why not, it's fun. But I'll never forget that first lesson as long as I live. It really made me think how important it is to God that husbands and wives love each other. I thought about my role in this passage and would I be willing to give up my life for my wife as Jesus did for His church? God has truly blessed me with a wonderful woman for my wife. I can't even imagine life without her, and I have learned a lot about God's love through her, and how much He loves me by blessing me with such a terrific wife. But could I lay down my life for my wife? Well, I hope the Lord never asks me to do this, but if He does, I can confidently say here, Yes I could. Thank you God for letting me lead that Ephesians Bible Study. Thank you God for teaching me this kind of love for my wife. Thank you God for Tracie. And thank you God for blessing our marriage everyday.

I would like to finish this chapter talking about those Bible names (oh no here I go again). All I want to say is this. I read a great book called "When God Whispers Your Name" by Max Lucado, by the way I think Max Lucado is an absolutely brilliant writer and would highly recommend you read any of his books. But back to "When God Whispers Your Name", Max says that when we go home to heaven we will get a new name that God has already picked out for us. This is Biblically told to us. I'm kind of glad to hear this, because when you have grown up with a name like mine, Greg Gregoris, you look forward to a change. I ask God for just one small favor. After being unsuccessful in trying to pronounce some of those funny Bible names, I ask you now Dear Lord, please don't rename me Nebuchadnezzar.

Chapter Six

Sunday School And The Wheel Of Fortune

I have to admit here that I hated Sunday school as a kid. I know hate is a strong word but I have to be honest, I hated it. My brother, my sister and I were the only kids on the block who went to Sunday school, and we never missed a week. We went every Sunday after Sunday. Let me now ask you this, why did we go every single Sunday? I would like you the reader to choose what you feel is the correct answer that best explains why we went every week:

a.) We couldn't wait to sing hymns like Jesus Loves Me, and The Old Rugged Cross
b.) We loved our Sunday school teachers
c.) We really got into the lesson plan each week
d.) We wanted to learn The Apostle's Creed
e.) OUR PARENTS MADE US GO

If you guessed "E", bingo you got it. I wanted to play baseball like the other kids. Our Sunday school class started at 11:00 AM just about the same time all of my "heathen" friends were hitting the school yard with their bats and balls. This drove me nuts. If God loves me so much why doesn't He make it rain every Sunday so the ballgames will be canceled and I won't feel so rotten being stuck in Sunday school. Or better yet, why doesn't God develop a Sunday school at home tape program. I would have loved that at home tape program.

I understood or let's just say I accepted the fact that I had to go to "normal" school Monday through Friday. But the weekends for a kid is playtime, and this Sunday school thing was seriously cutting into my playtime. As a kid I use to pray to God and ask

Him if He would please consider moving Sunday school to another day, like Tuesday. Then I would have had a great excuse for missing Sunday school class, I had "normal" school on Tuesday. I found God to be one tough negotiator. Actually I found God to be very "bullheaded" as a youngster. He certainly didn't move off His position very often, if at all. He kind of had that I know it all attitude. Oh well, since God won't give in let me try Mom.

My 6th and 7th grade years in Sunday school were not good ones. I was becoming very disruptive in class and enjoyed behaving that way. I don't know how my Sunday school teacher put up with me. I use to shoot rubber bands and paper clips at the girl playing the piano to mess her up during the hymn sing. My teacher would try to punish me by making me stand up and sing a solo. I would stand up and just laugh at her and then make funny noises to make the other kids laugh. I was out of control and the problem was that some of the other boys in my class started following my lead and became disruptive.

My behavior got to the point where my Sunday school teacher use to send me home. She would just kick me right out of class. Did you ever see those commercials where the used car salesman would tell the customer that the car they were thinking about buying was driven by a sweet little old lady who just drove it to church? I had one of those sweet little old ladies as a 7th grade Sunday school teacher, and even she was throwing me out of class. The only problem was I was glad to get thrown out and it became a game to me to see how fast I could get thrown out the following week. I lived close enough to the church that I could walk home, but I never went immediately home. I knew I would be in trouble with my parents. So I would walk up to the local convenience store which was around the corner and down the street from the church and wait there until noon. Then I would proceed home.

My Mom finally put an end to the Sunday school problems I was having. She said Greg, do you want to stop going to Sunday school? I screamed YES! She said OK, you don't have to go anymore. Thank you Mom, I love you. You're great Mom, you are definitely my favorite parent this week, and you're certainly more compassionate than God. He won't budge an inch from His viewpoints. I knew I should have come to you first. Then my Mom turned around and said these words to me, but be ready earlier next week because from here on out young man you will be going to church with me. Darn it, that's not what I wanted to hear. Did I mention that my Dad was my favorite parent that week.

Actually Mom made a great decision. Our church service started at 9:30 AM so I was out of church in time for my ballgames. And my Mom's desire to nourish and have her children mature in Christian doctrine was still taking place. It was a win-win situation. Good job Mom.

Let us now fast forward to last year and I am sitting in church when one of my good friends in the church asks if I could teach his Sunday school class next week? Without really thinking because I happen to like this person, I said yes. What ever happened to let me pray about it and I will get back to you? This was the second time I forgot to apply that sound principal. Next week I was going to be a substitute Sunday school teacher. "LORD HAVE MERCY."

All kids love substitutes, it's your job as a kid to tear the substitute apart. That's what being a kid is all about, having the God given opportunity to destroy a substitute teacher. What kind of pain have I just brought on myself? Wait, I know what's happening here. God is now paying me back for how I behaved in Sunday school. How did I know this? Because when I finally asked my friend what class did he teach, he told me the 5th and 6th graders and the majority of the class was <u>boys</u>. It was too late to ask for God's mercy. I was about to learn first hand what was meant by the "Wrath Of God." I believe I prepared my Will that week.

I did make one intelligent move in preparation for my debut as a Sunday school teacher. I asked my mother-in-law what should I do? My mother-in-law happens to be one of the most giving people I have ever met in my life. I am in awe of the way she gives of herself to help others, and it didn't hurt that she had taught Sunday school for 12 years. She gave me the best advice you could possibly get. She told me to over prepare, because if there is any dead time in the lesson you're <u>dead</u> <u>meat</u>.

When I arrived at church that day it was raining, as a matter of fact it had rained all weekend. Rainy weekends are a Sunday school teachers worst nightmare, because now these kids have been cooped up in a house and they're ready to explode. I nervously walked into a classroom of 16 kids and we were operating in a room built to handle 10. To say it was cramped is putting it mildly. When I arrived the boys in the class were playing a game I was not familiar with. They were taking off their baseball caps and throwing them with all their might at the kid sitting across from them. I believe the object of this game was to hit the other kid in the head so hard that brain damage would occur. They wouldn't let me play so I immediately stopped this game.

I opened up with prayer, but I was the only one who actually listened to it. The kids continued chatting while I was praying for them. I couldn't make out what they were saying, I think they were speaking in tongues. The lesson plan actually started out pretty well, which even I have to admit kind of surprised me. But now it was time to take the substitute teacher on. I was wearing one of my Lee Iacocca shirts as I call them. Lee Iacocca was famous for wearing blue shirts that had a white collar. I was wearing a red dress shirt with a white collar and a nice tie. Suddenly one of the boys in the class noticed something on my red shirt and he felt compelled to share this information with everybody. The boy stood up and said Mr. Gregoris, are you aware that your shirt now has big sweat stains under your arm pits. The class went wild. I taught the rest of the class with my hands down and my arms pinned to my sides. In other words I stopped pointing.

I thought I was in trouble now but my mother-in-law's advice was about to save me. Thank God I had over prepared for this lesson. I brought out something I created called Wheel Of The Bible. It was based off of Wheel Of Fortune, which I do watch on occasion. The kids just loved it, and they really got into it. I gave them a lesson plan which included locating different Bible verses, and then they had to write them in on a worksheet in their appropriate places. I then collected the worksheets and had all the correct answers covered on a large sheet of cardboard paper. Just like Wheel Of Fortune the kids gave me letters and then tried to solve the Bible puzzle. I would then give them bonus points if they could remember where in the Bible that verse could be found. Guess what people, I had survived my first Sunday school lesson. Thank you Pat and Vanna.

I have substituted as a Sunday school teacher three times since my first lesson, and it has been fun. But I also know that being a Sunday school teacher is not my calling. See pew-potatoes, I can say no. I have not been asked to be a regular Sunday school teacher by our church, but I would have to turn it down. I just don't feel the Lord is leading me in this direction.

We have one individual in my Bible Study who also happens to be a regular Sunday school teacher. He said something that really caught my attention and made me think. He said that he hoped he was reaching these kids, because sometimes it's so hard to tell. Most kids want to sprint (these sprinters make good pew-potatoes when they get older) out of Sunday school class when it's over and go hang out with their friends. I thought long and hard about this concern and I started thinking about my 7th grade Sunday school teacher. I don't know if she is even alive today and even if you did locate her and mentioned my name to her, she would probably think you were part of the prison fellowship mission that was trying to raise bail money to get me out of jail. I bet she would be surprised to hear that I got **involved** in church activities and even taught Sunday school. The point I'm trying to make is this. I think even my 7th grade Sunday school teacher had a positive impact on my life for Christ. Why else would I still be thinking about her.

It took me 25 years to finally learn my lesson (I'm a slow learner), but I now know what the Lord was trying to tell me through my 7th grade Sunday school teacher. The Lord was trying to get me to realize this truth about His love for me. Hold on to instruction, do not let it go; guard it well, for it is your life (Proverbs 4:13 NIV).

Personally, I think God looks down with great pleasure at what Sunday school teachers are doing every week all across the world. If I could give some words of encouragement to Sunday school teachers it would be this, keep planting those seeds in the kids mind. Take it from me the all-star pew-potato and Sunday school radical, someday that seed will be fertilized and blossom into a child of God who wants to get **involved** and help his church. GOD BLESS SUNDAY SCHOOL TEACHERS.

Chapter Seven

"The Angel Tree Project"
And George

I use to whine a lot (just ask my wife). As a matter of fact I kind of enjoyed whining and was pretty darn good at it. I could whine with the best of them. The Angel Tree Project was about to change that.

The Angel Tree Project is one of the best learning tools of what Christmas is all about that God could ever have placed in my life. Our church participates every year in the Angel Tree Project. The Angel Tree Project is one of our missions in the prison fellowship ministries that we support and our church's **involvement** in Angel Tree is led by two wonderful people, Dave Monie and Sandy Koch. There is no doubt in my mind that God is working through these two people in powerful ways.

The Angel Tree Project **involves** all of our church congregation in that we buy Christmas presents for children who currently have one of their parents in prison. These little kids really have it tough. They are either living with just one parent or they live with elderly grandparents. Most of the times these homes are in the inner city projects. The kids believe these presents are being sent to them from the parent who is incarcerated. That's the beauty of the Angel Tree Project. It's driven by love and a strong emotional desire to keep the family unit together.

My job was to be a driver. I was to drive to the different homes that were assigned to me and deliver the presents to the children, but the second part of my job was much more important. I was also there to see if there was anything our church could do to help them out, and to help them grow or begin their walk with Christ. I asked every household if the children were regularly attending a church in the local area. Every household I was in the guardian of the kids said "yes" they were attending a church. I hope they were telling me the truth. And if the guardian was not telling the truth I hope the Lord used that question to plant a seed in the guardian's mind on how important the church can be to a child growing up in a poverty and crime effected area. It can literally save the child in more ways than one.

One of the gifts we give to all the kids is a Children's Bible to help them learn and understand who Jesus is, and how much He loves them. The kids seem to love this gift the most. We also will normally purchase a toy and clothing items for the kids, but it's that Children's Bible that gets mentioned the most often when our church gets "thank you" letters written by the guardians or sometimes the kids themselves. I believe the children can write in these Bibles which I'm sure they really enjoy. Every little kid likes to write or draw inside a book especially when they think they're not allowed to. That makes it more fun, to see if you can get away with it. But in this case, they are encouraged to write in their new Bible.

I wish I could have written in a few Bibles. As a child I was kind of rebellious, I use to like to break some of the rules. What's that God, I was allowed to write in the Bible. You actually want me to write in my Bible. When did this happen? I thought it was a sin to write in the Bible. Why is this golden rule allowed to be broken? What's that God, it was never a rule. Well then why wasn't I informed about this sooner? I was. When? Oh, during 7th grade Sunday school after I had been thrown out. I sure am sorry I missed that.

I guess I learned something from these little kids. I am going to be just like them and write down my thoughts and my questions right in the Bible. Thanks for the lesson kids.

The Lord decided to teach me another lesson before my day had ended, and it's probably one of the best lessons God was ever going to teach me. I was in homes that I couldn't believe human beings were living in. I was in one home where they just had their heat turned off and everybody in the family (it was a large family) was now living in one room, the living room. They had bed sheets up blocking off the other rooms of the house so that they could keep all the heat in that one room. I was in another house where the night before there was a drug bust in the house. I asked if the children had witnessed this? The mother said yes. OUCH! We certainly need to pray for these children.

Here now is the lesson that God was about to teach me through The Angel Tree Project. What I just wrote about in the previous paragraph sounds pretty bad, doesn't it? Most people including myself do not have any idea how much God has blessed our lives. The Angel Tree Project woke me up to how many blessings God has poured into my life. Blessings that up until now, I was just taking for granted. Remember I told you in the beginning of this chapter that I like to whine, and that I'm good at it. Well, I don't whine anymore, at least not very often. I don't like even being around people who whine. I like to be around people who count their blessings and really understand that old adage; there goes I except for the grace of God. Think about it. I thought about that a lot when I was in these people's homes.

Let me now ask you this, did you get to choose your parents? No, God did that for you. As a matter of fact you and I had absolutely no say in this decision at all. And I thank God everyday for the terrific parents He gave me. My parents took "parenting" very seriously and provided for me a home full of love and security. That's the only difference between me and the little children of the Angel Tree Project.

It seems God wasn't through with me yet. He had one more lesson He needed to teach me. The Jr. Youth Group of our church also gets **involved** with the Angel Tree Project. They help deliver the gifts and the Angel Tree kids do seem to enjoy playing and talking with our kids. I'm always amazed at how you can throw a bunch of strange children into a room, and they instinctively know how to make friends and play together. Boy, if only the adult population could get this concept right. Maybe we should play more as adults, that must be the key. Didn't Jesus say something about our faith is to be like that of a child's. Apparently the guy knew what He was talking about, didn't He!

I stopped at this one house to deliver the presents and there was about 20 young men just hanging out in the street, and they were being loud. I had two girls from the youth group working with me and they kind of got scared (I don't blame them). They did not want to get out of the car. I told them that we had to. This answer surprised even me because it is my nature to be very protective. Trust me, I was quite surprised that my answer wasn't yeah, let's get out of here, we can always say they weren't home. It seems that God wouldn't let me leave. He wanted the girls and me to trust Him. I told the girls that God wanted us to go in there and that He would protect us. We were doing His work, so He would keep us safe. And that's exactly what happened. We got out of the car, got the presents out of the trunk, went up to the house, made the delivery, talked with the guardian, and got back into the car. All without any trouble whatsoever. I believe all those young men in the street just kind of knew we were there trying to do God's work and help this family.

The girls learned a valuable lesson that day, and that is to trust God with all the difficult situations that come up in life. Someone else also learned to trust God in difficult situations, the driver, ME!

When I think back upon this incident I have to laugh. It seems to be one of the few times God and I were on the same page when it came to decision making. I'm starting to feel a little better about that college I went to. But here's the funny part. My first reaction was to get out of there, but instead I did the opposite. It proves my point that God's plan always seems to work in reverse of my plans. The Bible says that even the wisest man's plans are foolish as compared to God's plans. I'm certainly not the wisest man on earth, I'm not even close, but I am living proof about the foolish plans part.

I have given God many laughs over the years when I developed my own plans without asking for His help to solve my difficult problems. I'm sure God laughed, and I'm glad He laughed. I'm also glad that God has a great sense of humor. How do I know that God has a great sense of humor? He created us didn't He. I don't think any more proof is necessary. Do you?

I sometimes feel like that George character on the TV show

Seinfeld, when I'm evaluating the way I want to do things as compared to the way God wants me to do things. George is the guy who just seems to be stumbling through life until this one episode when he makes this one great discovery. Since all of his thoughts and ideas produce disastrous results, he now decides he's going to do the complete opposite of everything he thinks is right. This opposite thinking becomes a gold mine for George and he starts to meet pretty women, gets a great job with the New York Yankees, and starts to develop more confidence in himself. So is this my answer, do I become the "Christian George" and do the complete opposite of what I think, and then God and I will live together in perfect harmony. I don't think so. I'll have to admit I am tempted to try it, but I think it would be a cop out and a major disappointment to the Lord.

My answer and maybe this is your answer too, is really quite simple. Just include God in all your decisions. The important word in the last sentence is **all**. God wants to help make decisions for us, so why not let Him. He never makes the wrong decision, can you say that? I know I can't. He even wants to help make the little decisions in our lives. In the book of Proverbs it says the following; in all your ways acknowledge him, and he will make your paths straight (Proverbs 3:6 NIV). It seems that no part of our life is considered to small for God. That's really "big" of Him, wouldn't you say.

I don't know about you, but I'm tired of paying for my wrong decisions. I have some really ugly ties that don't seem to match any of my suits, and I'm confident that God would have changed my decision when I bought those ugly ties if only I had asked Him. Am I saying that God should be making your shopping decisions? Why not. Go check out the wardrobe that you have hanging in the closet and remember this, God never makes the wrong decision. Next time you go to the Mall, start with a prayer, it can only help.

One last word about the Angel Tree Project. I think because of my **involvement** in Angel Tree the true meaning of Christmas has been revealed to me. It's a great thrill for me to watch the faces on the Angel Tree children as they open their presents which they believe is a gift from their parent who is in jail. It's important to them, because this gift shows that this parent still loves and cares about them. Their little faces just light up bright and explode into a great big smile. I imagine this was the same look on the faces of those shepherds when they saw the baby Jesus lying in the manger. And this should be the look on our faces, every Christmas morning. Come to think of it, shouldn't we have that kind of great big smile everyday of our lives? ABSOLUTELY! That smile is our way of telling the world that we belong to Jesus Christ.

Chapter Eight

Me A Presbyterian —
I Can't Even Spell Presbyterian

I currently attend Bunker Hill Presbyterian Church, and I love my church. I love the people in the church, I love the pastor, and I think our church is the greatest church in the world. And if you don't believe that about your church, shame on you. Even though I do believe that Bunker Hill is the greatest church in the world, it was a crooked path that got me here.

I was raised a Methodist and attended the Methodist church right up to my going away to college. I even went to church while I was in college, which at times wasn't easy. I was born and raised in New Jersey but I went to college in North Carolina. Scenery didn't mean a whole lot to me back then I was only 18, but North Carolina is absolutely one beautiful state. While I was there some of my college friends would ask me why I was going to church on Sunday? My parents weren't around to enforce this. Plus the fact that during my college years I definitely was not living the life or setting the example of a so-called Christian. It was my lifestyle that was most confusing to my friends. On any given Friday or Saturday night I was probably breaking six of the Ten Commandments, and if I was having what I considered a "great" weekend back in college, I probably pushed that number to as high as eight. Then I would march off to church on Sunday.

My college friends asked a good question. Why was I going to church on Sunday? Here was my response back then; I said that I go to church every Sunday because I feel like I have to be there, and because I get such a great feeling inside me after the worship service. I gave that answer some twenty years ago and I still wouldn't change it a bit if asked today. That's why I went. God wanted me there so He planted that in my mind, and I felt great afterwards because God had forgiven my sins. I'm sure He saw me breaking those eight commandments on a "great" weekend, but He still forgave me. Now that's what I call LOVE!

You have to trust me on this one, during my college years I was racking up some serious points in that sin category. Go right now and look in your Bibles where it says that the "flesh is weak" (Matt. 26:41 KJV), you will probably see my college photograph next to this verse giving you a visual example of this truth. If sin was a category on Jeopardy, I'm pretty sure during my college years I could've swept that whole category. Yes, Mr. Trebek, I'll take Sin for a $1000. But thank God for those church services and the work that Jesus did on the cross for me so that all my sins would be forgiven. It helped me get through college, even though I didn't realize it at the time.

After college I returned home to New Jersey, I started working but stopped going to church. Why did I stop going? I didn't feel like going anymore. Mom's and Dad's, how many times have you heard your twenty-two year old children say that line? I'll bet quite a bit. This lasted ten years for me. Oh, I went to church on Christmas Eve and Easter during this time, but that was it. I figured God loves me, right. I knew this to be true, so I rationalized that if God loved me and I was nice to other people I had all the angles covered as far as getting into heaven. Church was for people who didn't know how to be nice to other people, it wasn't for someone like me who was already a good guy and well liked by my peers. Plus, there's a bunch of hypocrites in the church. Who needs to be around those back stabbers.

As you can see I developed a brilliant defense on why I should stay at home on Sundays. God knew where I was at if He needed me. I was on the couch eating a pizza watching sports, what all men were born to do on Sundays. Unfortunately, some guys carry this tradition right through the week. Sorry about that ladies, but it's not our fault. This Sunday couch and sports thing is in our genes. It's an inherited gene that is passed down to us. So it's heredity that causes us men folk to act this way on Sundays. We are <u>helpless</u> to fight this ritual of life. I'm sure if there was football back in the Old Testament days, that Moses and the other men would have kicked back in their tents and ordered a pepperoni and mushroom manna and would have watched the game.

Whenever you ask someone why they don't go to church, the number one answer seems to be this; because there's a bunch of hypocrites in the church. The pastor at Bunker Hill Presbyterian Church has a great answer to that response. Our pastor's name is Mark Atkinson, and he is the greatest pastor in the world. And if you aren't saying the same about your pastor, shame on you. Here is Pastor Atkinson's reply to the hypocrite question; "yes", there are a bunch of hypocrites in our church, but we can always use one more. Is that a great answer or what.

So how did I get on this crooked path that would eventually lead me to a church and a denomination that I couldn't even spell. It started by my love for reading. I love to read, it is certainly one of my favorite hobbies along with sports. One summer day I was over my parent's house and I was talking to my sister. My sister and her husband were members of a Baptist church in their hometown, and both were getting very much **involved** in their church's activities. At the time I didn't think much of it, but I could tell that my sister's faith was certainly growing. I was telling her about some of the books I was reading and how fast I was getting through them. She then suggested to me that I read the Bible. Well this sounded like a challenge to me and one thing I won't run from is a challenge. So I decided that day to read the Bible.

My beginning efforts in reading the Bible were not good ones. First of all, I didn't know where my Bibles were hidden. I was practicing the new-age mandatory good housekeeping laws of keeping your Bibles out of sight. If you have your Bibles out on display, people will think you are a "Jesus Freak", and won't talk to you anymore. Can't have that can we? My second problem was that I started reading the King James Version and I severely struggled with the words (oh no, here I go again with that hang-up on Bible words).

I learned that the King James Version of the Bible was written in what is called Old English. Well, there was my problem. I'm not that old and I'm not English. Where did they get some of these words anyway? I was taught that Christ was the great communicator. If He was using these kinds of words I can now understand why the disciples always seemed a little baffled. If Jesus was speaking at a seminar today and was using these words, I would definitely be His biggest nuisance. I would be raising my hand after every sentence asking Him questions like this. Oh Jesus, my Dear Savior, it's me again, what does the words Ye, soweth, thence, doest, cometh, and thinkest mean, I can't seem to locate them in my Webster's New World Dictionary. I would be demanding that you give me one of those United Nations headsets where all the languages are translated into the language that I speak, "normal" everyday English. I need words that I can at least find in my pocket dictionary.

Let me prove my point here. This is the King James Version of Matthew 5:39; But I say unto you, That ye resist not evil: but whosoever shall smite thee on thy right cheek, turn to him the other also. If I had my U.N. headset on I believe this same verse from Jesus would have sounded like this; If someone busts up the right side of your face, turn and let him bust up the left side of your face. Now isn't that translation easier to understand. I believe in this verse that Jesus is counting on the guy to break his hand when he decides to get greedy and take that second punch at you. Actually this verse in the Bible under any translation has to be one of the most deeply compassionate teachings that our Lord gave us to follow.

It was now time for me to make an executive decision about trying to read the Bible. I then remembered that just before I went to college the church that I was a member of then, Colonial Manor Methodist Church, had given me as a gift The Living Bible for me to read at college. I picked up that Bible twice while I was in college. The first time was when I packed it to take it down with me my freshman year. The second time was my senior year, when I had to pack it to take it home with me. Besides those two occasions The Living Bible never saw the light of day.

Guess what happened next? I started reading The Living Bible and was enjoying it. This Bible was lying dormant for fourteen years and now it was going to shape my future. I even got to the point where I would let this Bible stay out on the coffee table in the living room where other people could actually see it. God was making me bold. I would highly recommend that if you are going to read the Bible and you have never done so before, that The Living Bible is an excellent Bible to start out with. So what are you waiting for? Get started reading.

After reading The Living Bible I knew I wanted to go back to church. I told my wife this and she also wanted this to happen for the both of us. Here was my criteria for choosing the church of my dreams. I wanted a big church, one that I could get lost in, and where I could just go to the Sunday worship service and be left alone the rest of the time. If this big church just happened to have side doors, all the better. Remember, side doors are excellent when you decide to use the "great escape" method (See Chapter Two). Was I a major league pew-potato or what!

I now set out to find this perfect church for my wife and I. We decided to visit two local churches and see which one we liked the best. Denomination wasn't important to me, being left alone was. My wife who was raised a Presbyterian felt some loyalty to them I guess, so the second church we were going to visit was this church called Bunker Hill Presbyterian Church.

The first church we visited was big, and the service was well done but people wanted to talk with me afterwards. I didn't get out in time. All pew-potatoes know that feeling, it's worst than death. You have missed timed the pastor ending the Benediction and now you're stuck mingling with people who are trying to get you on their church committee. So it was a no-go with the first church we visited. Why? Because they'll probably want me to do something. When I look back at this today, I'm sure God had to be cracking up about my criteria for choosing a church. I don't think this was the criteria the apostles had in mind when they were starting up the churches. I sure hope that when the Lord calls me home the apostles don't try to flogg me.

The second church we visited was Bunker Hill Presbyterian Church, and at first I didn't like it. I had only been in the church two minutes when I declared to my wife that this church is too small. This is not the right church for us. Everybody will know our business. If we miss church one week, everybody will want to know where we were, and what was wrong? Let's time the Benediction right this week and get out of here quick. It was now God's turn to start doing some powerful work.

The service was fantastic that day and I felt the sermon was written for me. God had remarkably changed my attitude in one hour. I missed timed the Benediction again, except now I didn't seem to care. When I got out of the church I looked at my wife and said, we're coming back aren't we? She smiled and said "yes." We have been coming back for five years now. Wow, when my wife says "yes", she really means it. God wanted us at this church and my wife and I could just sense that. I wish I could accurately explain this feeling to everybody, but I just can't. People who are mature in their faith know what I mean when I tell them about this powerful feeling that came over us. I just knew this is where God wanted us to be. I knew we were going to become a part of this church, and we both knew this after our first visit.

The first valuable lesson I was going to learn from my new church was about prayer. One key message that Bunker Hill Church strives to communicate is for each of us to develop a "personal" relationship with our God. I needed to learn this in my prayer life. Let me explain. I use to like to use the word beseech a lot when I prayed. I know this is hard to believe because I hate all those funny Bible words. But it sounded religious to me, so I naturally thought God would like it and answer more of my prayers. I asked God to beseech me this, to beseech me that, to beseech me everything. I figured God was up there in heaven just beaming with pride every time I said the word beseech. Then God played a trick on me. He decided to test me on this word and the conversation went like this:

God: Greg

Greg: Yes God

God: What does the word beseech mean?

Greg: I don't know God

God: Well then STOP using it!

Greg: But I thought You liked the word beseech, it's in the Bible, it's one of those religious words.

God: I do like the word beseech. But not from you!

Greg: But why?

Then God gave me the most beautiful answer I have ever heard in my life. God said; Greg my precious child, I love you just the way you are. I created you that way. Talk to Me like Greg Gregoris would talk. I understand you better that way. I just ask Greg, that you talk to Me often. I love you My child.

Now go ahead and substitute your name in place of mine. If you're like me it will bring tears to your eyes.

I now pray differently than I did before. I talk to God the same way I would talk to my best friend. I don't use the word beseech anymore because that's not how I talk. I'm not saying there is anything wrong with using big words when you speak to God if that is a part of your everyday vocabulary. It's just not a part of my vocabulary and God knew it. Now that my communication difficulty with God has been solved I definitely feel my prayers are being heard and answered in a more timely fashion. It's good to be down right personal with God.

Let's get back to our Bible reading, shall we. The Bible that our church uses is the New International Version (NIV) and I've come to really enjoy reading out of this Bible. The scholars did a great job of translating this Bible. I do have to say one thing in the King James Version's defense, and that is this. The 23rd Psalm in the King James Version is one of the most beautiful pieces of written literature the world has ever known. I'm extremely pleased that scholars decided to make translations of the King James Bible, but there should be a law that you are not allowed to tamper with the 23rd Psalms. That should stay the same in any Bible.

My wife and I joined Bunker Hill Presbyterian Church about a year and a half ago, so we are now members. I guess this means we'll have to show up at the congregational meetings and dinners. I hope they don't serve peas at these dinners. I just can't eat those peas. I have even learned how to spell Presbyterian, how about that. I'm proud to be a Presbyterian, but I'm even more proud of being a Christian. And did I mention that our church is the greatest church in the world.

Chapter Nine

A Little TLC (Too Little Cash)

Sorry, I'd sure like to help out, but I'm already giving all that I can. That's what I would like to tell my church when it comes time to deliver on my financial pledge for our new building expansion program. This would not send a very positive sign to our congregation, especially since I am in a position of leadership being chairperson of the Capital Stewardship Committee (more about this responsibility in the next chapter). I can just hear the people screaming that if the chairperson isn't willing to give more why should I? I sometimes wonder why God just doesn't rain down money on us like He did with the manna for the Israelites in the desert during Moses time. Boy, it sure seems to me that God was a lot more generous back then, doesn't it?

Our church desperately needs a new building and God knows we need this new building. We need this building to continue to effectively teach the Gospel and expand with our growing community. The only thing stopping us from starting right now is, "the money." So come on God, get with the program, where are those pennies from heaven we keep praying for? And when you factor in inflation, plus the interest rate the bank wants to charge us, the heck with those pennies, we need dollars from heaven.

I thought our situation was unique in that we are blessed with an abundance of young children in our church, but the timing may not be right for us to start this massive project. After contemplating this situation for a while I am convinced that there is no such time as the right time or the perfect time. There is <u>always</u> a reason for not starting something that will require hard work or sacrifice. I myself, have used excuses many of times to avoid beginning a particular project.

Every year I've been saying that I am going to finish and fix up my basement. Well, I've been telling my wife this for at least five years now. And if you were to ask me today, Greg, when are you going to finish your basement? I would calmly answer, I'm going to get to that "next year." What a nice safe answer. I am going to do that next year. Next year is going to be a better year, I can just feel it. And this cycle keeps continuing proving the point that there is no such thing as the perfect time to get started.

So now I had to asked myself this challenging question, is this the right time for our church to start raising money for our future or should we wait another year and pray about it some more? I understand from some wiseman that next year is going to be a better year. Well God provides some pretty clear advice to us Christians about praying upon such difficult matters. First, it is right and good to pray to God about all things. Second, when the cause is right with God and He has heard your prayer, it's now time to get into immediate action.

I love this particular verse in The Living Bible because I can just vision God saying this to Moses. The verse I'm referring to is Exodus 14:15, and at this moment in time the Israelites are trapped against the Red Sea and Moses is praying like crazy for some kind of divine help. The verse reads like this; Then the Lord said to Moses "Quit praying and get the people moving! Forward, march! (Exodus 14:15 The Living Bible). If we humans were speaking for God back then I believe our response to Moses would have been a little bit different and sounded more like this; Hey Moses you lazy load, just "shut up" and get into action. What in the world are you waiting for, I heard you the first time. What do you think I am, deaf or something! Get your butt moving Moses or I'll replace you with your brother Aaron. The point I hope I have driven home here is that yes our Lord definitely wants us to pray to Him about everything, but He also requires action from us when our prayers are answered.

It seems to me that our God does not find favor in the one trait we humans seem to have gotten down to a science. That trait being procrastination. Most people I know, including myself, are very clever at finding ways and developing bullet proof strategies to delay doing jobs that we find difficult, time consuming or boring. Let's be honest here, if my choices are playing golf this afternoon or painting the church, I'll choose golf ten out of ten times (unless somebody can prove to me that painting the church would improve my putting). I'm positive I could convince myself and others that it would be wiser to paint the church "next year" because we will have more new members to help out on this project. Now that my friends is a great pew-potato answer to getting out of work. The only problem with this great pew-potato answer is that it shows a lack of personal discipline, poor time management skills, and in some cases is actually disobedient to God.

That's a strong statement made in the above paragraph. But ponder on this point for a moment; is it possible our delay tactics that we have all mastered over the years could in reality be considered disobedient to God? I believe so! A good example of this in the Bible is when Joshua is asking some of the Israelite tribes why they haven't taken the land God has already promised them (Joshua 18:3). Joshua makes it very clear to these tribes that God has heard their prayers, so they are to stop procrastinating and go forward taking possession of the land that the Lord had promised them. This same message delivered by Joshua in the Old Testament holds true today. We should all take heed of Joshua's sound advice the next time we are confronted with a difficult task or lengthy project that we know in our hearts must get done.

I would like to go back to the story of Moses and the Israelites because there is a valuable lesson we can learn from it. As rebellious as the Israelites sometimes were out there in the desert, there were other times when they gave fully of themselves to the Lord. Also, the Bible is very clear and leaves no doubt that their giving pleased our Lord immensely. I have got to believe at this specific time in history the Israelites could have easily of justified that it was not the "right time" to have to give anymore then they had already given. I mean think about it for a minute, these Israelites had already given over 400 years in bondage. That bondage thing sounds like a sufficient sacrifice to me. You just can't ask these people to give anymore of themselves, right? Wrong!

It must of took a lot of courage, but Moses asked the whole

Israelite community to make an offering of their possessions so that they could build the Tabernacle (Exodus 35). How did this group of people respond to Moses request? The Israelites responded with tremendous generosity to this special offering to the Lord. The Bible records the following of this blessed event; "No man or woman is to make anything else as an offering for the sanctuary." And so the people were restrained from bringing more, because what they already had was more than enough to do all the work (Exodus 36:6-7 NIV). WOW! Did these people totally understand the concept of the "joy of giving" or what! Can you imagine your pastor or better yet one of those TV evangelist getting into the pulpit and begging people to stop sending in their money because they have "too much" of it and they don't know what to do with it all. I have yet to hear my pastor say those words (stop giving so much) and I seriously doubt I ever will.

Ron Blue, in his excellent book entitled Storm Shelter, says that we find financial freedom only when we learn to give freely. Ron goes on to say that if he could proclaim only one message, this would be it: Everything we have belongs to God. When we give, all we are doing is demonstrating this fact.

Ron further states in his book that recognizing God's ownership of all our resources (including our money) is probably the single biggest key to financial freedom. His book validates the point that giving breaks the power that money sometimes has over us.

I would like to go back to the beginning of this chapter where I stated in the very first paragraph that I am already giving all that I can. I now have come to realize after reading the Bible about the plight of the Israelites in the desert that my answer won't hold up in God's eyes. I also know that God decides when it is the "right time" to get into action, not me. So there goes my built in alibi of saying I'll do it next year.

At this particular time in my life it looks like my family is going to need a new car. As I'm sure you are aware of, a brand new automobile is certainly not cheap these days. So I just started saving some money for a new car and "now" my church wants me to make a three year financial commitment to our new building fund . How many of you can relate to this situation? Does God have some awful timing or what?

So what is the answer my friends? Can I give my church the same answer that I give my wife about finishing the basement? Come back and see me next year, I'm sure next year will be a better year. I don't think so. This response will also fall woefully short in God's eyes. Here is what I firmly believe God would say to all Christians about when is the right time to sacrifically give; There is no such thing as the "right time." The right time is right now.

Finally, let's take a look at this from an investment point of view. What is the return you can expect to receive from your financial investments to your church? Does God function like a bank and has a Christmas Club set up in heaven that will return our money to us every December? And if this is true, I would hope and pray that Judas Iscariot is not the administrator of this fund (see Matt. 25:14-16 for my reasons of concern). The ultimate return you can expect to receive is something no Wall Street broker or bank could ever guarantee you. The Bible says that if your profits are in heaven your heart will be there too (Matt. 6:21 The Living Bible). Your return from God and His church is not a monetary return, but instead is the guarantee of heavenly treasures where they can never lose their value. Now that's an investment worth making.

Chapter Ten

From Pew-Potato To Committee Chairperson (God Help Us All)

I received a phone call one night that kind of shocked me. I was asked if I would accept the position of Committee Chairperson of the Campaign Fund Committee. What was happening here? I was going from pew-potato to Committee Chairperson is that legal? Apparently it is, I think it's covered in one of Jesus' beatitudes. I believe Our Savior said; Blessed be the pew-potato for he will one day be in charge of something. I forget what Gospel this is written in, so you'll just have to look it up yourselves.

FINALLY, I gave the right answer to this person's request. I said, let me pray about it and I will get back to you. Good job Greg. My initial gut reaction to this request of being a chairperson was to say no thank you. Why take this headache on, right? Well it seems that God had a different gut reaction than I did. He told me through my prayers to accept this responsibility, and that He would guide me. I called the person back and accepted my new position of Campaign Fund Chairperson.

My first question was, what does the Campaign Fund Committee do? What's its job? Here is my layman's answer to this question. Our committee's job is to bug people for money. We have since changed our name to the Capital Stewardship Committee, and what is the role of the Capital Stewardship Committee? To bug people for money.

I believe another fringe benefit we received for changing our committee's name was that we got to use the nicer church stationery. Hey, don't laugh. You need the best stationery you can get your hands on when you go asking for more money.

Our church has a problem right now, but it's a problem we gladly welcome. The problem that God has blessed us with is that we have outgrown our present facility. This is especially true in our Sunday school area. We have been blessed with an abundance of children and our church is thankful for that. We also take our community responsibility of providing quality Sunday school lessons very seriously. So because of these reasons it's now time for our church to get started on a building expansion program.

Once again I was confused at God's rationale of choosing me for this position of chairperson. This choice rubs in the face of any prudent business person. Think about it. If I were to make a business decision as important as putting someone in charge of a committee, my first criteria would be experience. How much prior experience does this person have to draw upon to do the job right. That makes sense, doesn't it?

How much experience do I have in capital stewardship? Absolutely none. Zero. I have never done anything remotely similar to what I was about to attempt. So here are the qualifications I had to offer the congregation of our church about my ability to produce successful results. NONE! That's right people. I have no experience in this stewardship stuff and to top it off, I honestly confess here that I don't know what I'm doing. I have never been in charge of a committee in my life. NEVER! How about that for building supreme confidence and a positive attitude among the congregation.

Any good business person will tell you that you can overcome an inexperience leader by surrounding them with an experience staff. God did surround me with a committee and I am thankful for every one of them. So how much experience in capital stewardship did my committee people have? Absolutely none. Zero. That's right, you read that correctly, they had none.

So let's examine what we have here. We have a committee staff who has absolutely no experience in what we're about to do in the area of capital stewardship. Plus the fact this staff is completely loyal to the leader (me) who also has no experience in capital stewardship and freely admits that he doesn't' know what he's doing.

If I sent this on a resume to your church, would you hire us to be your Capital Stewardship Consultants? NO! Why not? I'm deeply insulted. Keep reading because I'm about to show you why every church in the world should hire our happy, I don't know what I'm doing committee. You see, we've learned the secret.

I will concede here that no business person in there right mind would hire me or our committee. But remember what I said earlier about the wisest man's plans as compared to God's plans. Maybe a sharp business executive wouldn't hire our group, but we don't care. We found someone who was glad to hire us, Almighty God. And He got us at a very reasonable price.

The dollar amount that our church will have to raise should be in the seven figure range by the time we get finished building. Do I feel this inexperienced staff and their I don't know what I'm doing leader will be successful? You Bet I Do! Absolutely! I'm 100% Confident! No Doubt In My Mind! But how? Glad you asked.

I'm totally serious about our church being extremely successful in raising the necessary capital for our building expansion. The staff on the committee and myself have come up with the greatest plan in the world to accomplish our goal. I'm going to share this plan with you, so right now go and get a piece of paper and a pencil to write down this amazing success formula. Here it is; **FAITH**. That's all we ever really needed.

A pastor by the name of Sam Boyes, who use to speak at our church every so often when we were searching for a new pastor, taught me a terrific way to understand what faith means. This is what he showed me:

Forsake
All
I
Trust
Him

Pretty good lesson, wouldn't you agree? Thank you Reverend Sam.

You see the reason I know that our church is going to be

successful is because who is going to get all the glory for this great and worthy accomplishment. You can't give the glory to the committee staff, they don't have any experience in this particular area. And you certainly can't give me any of the glory as the leader, I have already gone on record saying that I don't know what I'm doing. I have no experience in capital stewardship or in running a committee. I have never done anything like this before. So then, who gets the glory for this wonderful achievement. God gets all the glory, just as it should be.

Some people believe that God has stopped doing miracles since the Bible was written. I know that's wrong. God is still performing miracles today. He's taken an all-star pew-potato like me and now has me in a leadership position of a very important committee. Trust me, that's a miracle. Let's not forget it was only a couple of years ago when my number one church requirement was to be left alone. I'm enjoying working on this committee and in my opinion that's another miracle. I just always assumed church work to be totally boring. Well it's not. It's actually exhilarating at times, and I believe that qualifies as another miracle. So you see God is still performing miracles, you just have to look for them.

There is one message I would like to make clear here to my fellow pew-potatoes. Don't make the same mistake that I did, by just assuming that I didn't have enough talent in a particular area to get the job done properly. Don't ever be afraid to volunteer for something because of a lack of talent. I found out that's not a good enough reason. You see God is right now teaching me an incredible lesson through this committee. Whenever I have lacked the talent to be an effective leader of this committee, God was always there to lend me His. He will do the same for you. That's His promise and God always keeps His promises.

I have to admit to one little white lie I kind of wrote about in this chapter. I said throughout this chapter that I didn't know what I was doing while I was running our committee. That's not all together true. I was doing one thing that was extremely intelligent. I was and still am praying to the Lord every night to guide every detail of our committee's work and to help us make good decisions. Then I thank the Lord for giving me the opportunity to serve Him, and for surrounding me with a dedicated committee staff. Now you know why I'm so sure our church will succeed in this campaign. God's in complete control. So let me finish with a simple rule to follow in case your church places you in a leadership role. Without God <u>nothing</u> is possible. With God <u>everything</u> is possible. From here on out I've decided to work with God on everything I do. How about you?

Chapter Eleven

The Church Golf Classic Part I

The strangest thing happened to me one Sunday morning in church. I was in the hallway when a good friend asked me if I would be interesting in playing in a church golf outing? I didn't even have to think about this one. Did you say GOLF! Of course I'll play. Count me in. Little did I know that no church golf tournament even existed at the time. My friend then asked me the following question; you play golf, don't you? I said yes. He then said "great", you're the Chairman of the Golf Committee. My church friend was smart, he didn't even give me a chance to say, let me pray about it and I'll get back to you.

So my friend then wrote on a piece of paper that we were going to have a church golf outing and gave it to the pastor to read as an announcement from the pulpit. Our pastor read the announcement and we immediately had people in the congregation who wanted to play. Guess what? We now have a golf tournament to organize.

This actually turned out to be a very enjoyable tournament to organize and run. I got a tremendous amount of help from two close friends of mine in the church (Dave MacKnight & Bill "Fuzzy" Rowe), and the tournament went off smoothly. As a matter of fact our first tournament went so well, that we are currently planning our second golf outing, The Church Golf Classic Part II - "THE SEQUEL."

We are hoping to double the number of players we had last year so that we can have twice as much fun. It's important to note here that "talent" is not required for our church golf tournament. If anyone has ever played miniature golf, and got their ball through the "Windmill Hole," they easily qualify for our tournament.

This was not a difficult committee to be on so if your church has something similar to this available, jump on the opportunity to help out you pew-potatoes. This is a good place to begin and get your feet wet in getting **involved** with your church. You'll also have some fun at the same time. We held all of our golf committee meetings (which totaled one) at a local restaurant.

I would love to tell you about some dazzling golf shots that we hit in our tournament, but nobody hit one. Here are the two most interesting stories that occurred on this day. First, one member of our congregation who shall remain nameless (it wasn't me), hit so many balls into the woods that the County Forest Ranger slapped him with a couple of tickets for cruelty to animals and littering. Second, we had one golfer in my foursome (again it wasn't me) who hit a tee-shot on the 18th hole that landed on the green of the 7th hole. The only problem was there was already a foursome on the green putting when the ball landed on top of their heads. Think about that for a second you golfers. One minute you are lining up a two foot birdie putt to beat all of your buddies out of their money, then the next minute you have to suddenly run for your life. No one got hurt, thank God. We are considering that it be made mandatory that hard-hats be worn by all players for this year's tournament.

Can you tell by what I have written that we had a blast at our church golf outing, which leads me to this point. I'm always amazed at the people who think Christians don't or can't have fun. Who is spreading this false rumor anyway? It's got to be Satan. Some of the most fun loving and humorous people I know, I met through our church. The Bible even tells us to be of good cheer (Acts 27:22 KJV). Hey, if it's in the Bible it has to be legal and good for us, right? So we Christians are just trying to follow that good cheer piece of advice that God gave us in Holy Scripture. Give this answer to your "heathen" friends and then watch their reaction.

I wonder why people have the impression that Christians just hang out praying all day (though that's not a bad idea). They really miss the point that God wants us to have fun in our lives. How do I know that God wants us to have fun? Just look at His son Jesus for the answer. Christ could have chosen any twelve people He wanted to become His disciples. They could have been Kings or highly respected religious leaders, but that's not what He did. Instead He chose twelve ordinary guys like you and me. People who at times could definitely screw things up, but had a lot of fun while they were doing it.

You would have to bet that Peter the "fisherman" took some serious razzing from the other "fishermen" disciples after he went out to meet Christ on the water and started to sink and drown. I don't know about you, but when I think of a professional fisherman, I just naturally assume he would be pretty good at handling himself in or around water. Can't you just hear the other "fishermen" disciples getting on Peter's case for dropping like a anchor once he stepped out of the boat. I can just picture Andrew, Peter's brother, rubbing salt into the wound by suggesting to Peter that he would give him lessons on how to do the "doggie paddle" just in case Peter falls into the water again. In Holy Scripture, Jesus refers to Peter as the rock (John 1:42, The Living Bible). I wonder now if it was because he sank like one?

Who do I think would be encouraging this kind of "horseplay" behavior? Jesus himself, that's who. I'm sure Christ knew laughter was very important for the bonding of His twelve dedicated workers. We have a name we put on this type of bonding today, it's called fellowship. Guess what's the number one driving force behind the success of our church golf outing? You got it, FELLOWSHIP!

So if your church doesn't have something like our golf tournament why don't you be the one to start one up. It doesn't necessarily have to be a golf tournament, it could be anything you want it to be. You just read how easy it was to start one up in our church, our pastor read an announcement from the pulpit, and that was it. So go ahead and try it, just try it, you have nothing to lose. Trust me on this one. I'll be willing to bet that your church will respond as enthusiastically as ours did.

The only other tiny problem that surfaced after our first golf outing was that our church insurance company got wind of how bad (inconsistent) we played and heard we almost killed four people, not to mention how many squirrels we sent scurrying for cover after sending shot after shot into the woods peppering their little homes. Our church insurance company has threatened to drop us if we hold the tournament this year. Wait a minute, they're messing up our good cheer message. We can't let them get away with that, can we? Of course not, we don't need those wimps. I'm sure there are millions of other insurance companies looking for "high risk" customers like us. I told you we Christians love to have fun. This insurance matter will probably be the next committee I get assigned to. FORE!

Chapter Twelve

"Exhortation," But I Want To Speak In Tongues!

If it wasn't bad enough learning how to spell Presbyterian, God had another trick up His sleeve for me. When you become a new member at our church one of the first things the pastor has you fill out is this worksheet entitled Unwrapping Your Spiritual Gifts. It's an evaluation sheet designed to help you identify and develop your God given spiritual gifts. Personally I didn't think I had any spiritual gifts. I was pretty good in football when I was younger but our church doesn't have a football team so there's not much God could really do with me, right? I'm almost positive the Bible doesn't list playing football as one of God's spiritual gifts, unless God decided to use my kicking ability. I was the punter on my freshman football team. God could use my punting skills if some-one in the balcony of our church forgot their Bible, I could fetch one of the extra Bibles from our church narthex and then kick it up into the balcony.

It turns out that I was right about football not being one of God's spiritual gifts, and the pastor told me he would get quite upset if I started kicking Bibles around the church. So it looks like I have nothing special to offer the Lord. Apparently I'm the one person on this earth who has no spiritual gifts. I guess this means I can go back to being a full time pew-potato.

Wrong again Greg. According to Scriptures everyone of us has a special ability (spiritual gift) that God has placed inside of us (1 Cor.12:4-11). I understand that one way to really make God annoyed at you is to ignore or not utilize your special gift. Time out here! If I don't know what my spiritual gifts are, how can God possibly be mad at me? It's not like it was printed on my birth certificate, and my high school and college did not offer courses on discovering your spiritual gifts. That means it's totally impossible to learn what my spiritual gifts are. Wouldn't you agree?

It seems God did provide a way to learn about your spiritual gifts and it's a relatively simple procedure. What is this simple procedure you might ask? Reading your Bible daily. That's how God speaks and conveys information to us, through His word. Pray to God just before you read the Bible, that God will give you insight and understanding on what you're about to read. Ask the Lord to make His message clear to you, so that you can begin to apply it in your daily life. I personally just started doing this and I feel results are already beginning to spring forward. If you will start to do this, you will be well on your way to discovering and displaying the spiritual gift that God has placed inside of you.

As I stated earlier I came upon my spiritual gift another way, by answering questions on a spiritual gift evaluation sheet. The results from this evaluation clearly indicated that my spiritual gift was something called "exhortation." Thank you Lord, You have blessed me with a gift that I have no idea what it means, plus I can't even pronounce or spell it. Dear Lord, are you still punishing me for my behavior in 7th grade Sunday school? I said I was sorry!

A good question to ask right now is why did I totally believe in the accuracy of this evaluation? I knew this evaluation was accurate when I saw that my score for the spiritual gift of music was a zero. A zero on this evaluation worksheet meant, "not at all." You only need two words to adequately describe my singing ability, and those two words are; it stinks. I can't even sing well in the shower, that's how bad it is. As soon as I saw my zero in music I knew this evaluation had me pegged.

It was now time for me to go to the Lord in prayer. I thanked God for revealing my spiritual gift to me and asked Him if I could make a trade. I asked the Lord if I could trade this exhortation thing for the ability to speak in tongues. I just think that would be so neat to be able to speak in tongues. I know actually where I could use this special gift. In my next presentation for the Capital Stewardship Committee (the committee that's allowed to use the church's best stationery) I would slip into speaking in tongues and my interpreter (who would naturally be a committee member) would say God is telling the church through Greg that our committee needs an extra $10,000 dollars in our budget immediately. Wow, would I know how to use this powerful gift or what?

Apparently God can read minds and knew I would be dangerous with this particular spiritual gift. God certainly did hear my prayer and He gave me a quick and decisive answer. He said, NO! I knew I should have went to Mom first. Oh well, it looks like I'm stuck with that exhortation thing, whatever that is.

I looked up the word exhortation in the dictionary and to my surprise here is what it said about my new found spiritual gift: Exhortation — The ability to minister words of encouragement, consolation, comfort and motivation. To be able to help others complete their tasks.

I don't know about you, but that sounds pretty good to me. Thanks God. I assume this gift will come in handy when we start our new building expansion program. I guess it will be my job to cheer on the construction workers. Way to go guys, way to hammer that nail in. Good hit, right on the head of the nail. Way to measure guys, that almost fits, good try, I'm sure we can hide that one. "Let's Go" construction team we're right behind you. Two, Four, Six, Eight, build us a church that's really "great." Okay, I'll stop showing off my spiritual gift now.

I think I have been subconsciously applying my spiritual gift for some time now. I'll give you an example. I play golf with a very dear and close church friend of mine. Well this dear and close church friend of mine routinely kicks my butt on the golf course. Since I have discovered my spiritual gift I now can accurately explain why this keeps happening. I am actually "exhorting" my dear and close church friend by building up his confidence and self esteem with each victory. Here's the funny part, he thinks he's winning because he is better than me. The jokes on him, but if that's what he wants to believe that's fine with me. Remember my job is to "exhort" him to be all that he can be.

It's not only important to use our spiritual gifts (remember God gets annoyed if we ignore them) but apparently there is a certain way we are to display these special abilities that God has granted us. All of our special abilities are to be used in serving others, and none are for our own exclusive enjoyment. I know this sounds kind of hypocritical coming from a person who wanted to abuse the speaking in tongues gift, but it's the truth. So where did I, a potentially dangerous spiritual gift abuser, come up with this conclusion? The Bible.

The best way for me to explain this to you is to hand it over to the apostle Peter and read what he had to say about how to use our spiritual gifts. Here's what he said; Each one should use whatever gift he has received to serve others, faithfully administering God's grace in its various forms (1 Peter 4:10 NIV). So there it is, the apostle Peter is encouraging us to not only find our spiritual gifts, but also to put them to good use for the work of the church and the glory of God.

It's important for all of us to remember that after Christ ascended into heaven our role in God's plans changed dramatically. We now have inherited the job of becoming God's powerful instruments to relay His messages of hope and eternal salvation to the masses. That's an important responsibility my friends. The only training facility that I'm aware of who can prepare you for this responsibility is your local church. And just showing up on Sunday's won't make the grade. You have to get more involved in what goals your church is trying to accomplish if you want to thoroughly prepare yourself to have a positive influence on another individual. It's through you and me that God has chosen to reveal Himself to the non-believer. Now don't you feel more important and good about yourself knowing that God wants you on His team? I know I do.

It was now time for the Lord to show me a way on how I could express the gift of exhortation without sounding like a cheerleader, and that way was through prayer. I am on a prayer group that prays for our pastor. In the beginning I thought this was all backwards. I always thought that it was the pastor's job to pray for us, the congregation. Isn't that what we pay him to do? After the Sunday worship service he has all that time in the world on his hands, right? So from Monday through Saturday shouldn't he be praying for us? Shouldn't he be asking that God will bless us and make us rich and not strike us with lightening bolts when we screw up. That sounds like a normal pastor's duty to me. God then decided to teach me a valuable lesson about the shepherd He has chosen to lead our church.

Apparently the pastor needs just as many prayers as we do, and even more. Let me remind you of what I said in Chapter One about those fancy religious schools with the big crosses on them that all pastors attend. Those fancy religious schools with the big crosses on them leave in the "human frailties" part for the poor pastor to deal with on their own. In other words, the pastor is just like you and me when it comes to being tempted by sin. I now completely understand why we need to pray for our pastors. Our pastors are fighting the same exact battle that we're fighting.

I ask you to think about this scenario, where do you think Satan would attack first in his efforts to destroy God's Kingdom? The most logical answer has to be the church. If Satan could destroy the church, he would have effectively cut off God's network here on earth. And who runs our churches? Who oversees God's glorious network that the apostle's established and died for here on earth? Our pastors, that's who. So it makes perfect sense that Satan would attack our pastors first and hit them with all the power he has. If Satan can topple the "Big Chief" in the church, it's a good bet the rest of that church is in trouble also. A recent example of this would be what happened to the ministries of both Jim Bakker and Jimmy Swaggart. Once they succumbed to the temptations of Satan their whole organization was effected by it.

So now you can see why God is using my spiritual gift of exhortation to pray for our pastor. I pray to the Lord that He will protect our pastor from any attacks that Satan might be planning to use against him. I pray that the Lord will dress our pastor in His armor of defense to successfully ward off all of Satan's efforts. Here's where the exhortation part comes in, I then ask the Lord to completely fill our pastor with energy, enthusiasm, hope, and love that comes directly from heaven, and that God will use him in powerful ways to open the hearts and minds of our congregation and visitors to receive Christ as their personal Lord and Savior, and that he our pastor will continue to learn and grow in his own walk with the Lord. I pray that our pastor's words will touch the needs of all who hear his words, and that this Sunday's message will be the best message (I ask this every Sunday) that he has ever delivered. I then pray that at the end of the day when all is said and finished, that our Lord will look down upon our pastor and say these words to him; "well done my good and faithful servant."

This concept of a layman praying for the pastor no longer seems backwards to me, but now I actually consider it rewarding. It's amazing to me that when I'm praying with our pastor in his office right before the Sunday worship service begins, how powerful and emotional the prayers tend to be. You just know God is in the room listening. It's one of the greatest feelings I have ever experienced in my life. This is a great way for you to get **involved** with your church. Start praying for your pastor today, it <u>will</u> make a difference.

So since my gift is exhortation and the apostle Peter urged us to serve others with our gift I guess it's time for me to exhort you the reader. So here it goes. I first want you to accept this truth that applies to us all; what you are right now is only a shadow of what you can become once you accept Christ into your life. I urge you now if you haven't already, to accept Jesus Christ into your life and start exposing your spiritual gift for all the world to see. I urge you to get **involved** with your church's activities and help your church grow, they desperately need quality people just like you. Lastly, I urge you to help your pastor, you can and you will make a difference in your pastor's life. Your prayers of confidence and support for your pastor will certainly keep Satan <u>entirely</u> out of your church building. That's the kind of awesome power Almighty God has selected to place inside of you. That's right, you!

I now exhort you to take up the following challenge (I am currently taking this challenge on myself) and that is to go to church every Sunday, even when you are on vacation. Apparently it's very important to God that you are there each Sunday, no matter where you are. I think this Bible passage best illustrates the point; But the hour cometh, and now is, when true worshippers shall worship the Father in spirit and in truth; for the Father <u>seeketh</u> such to worship Him (John 4:23 KJV). I always thought there was a vacation exclusion or escape clause somewhere in Proverbs. It seems this verse from the Gospel of John in the New Testament is now the new covenant we have to follow, disallowing that Proverbs verse that I just can't seem to find at the moment. Oh well, I guess when Jesus said; this is the new covenant, He really meant it!

P.S. - After reading my challenge, if you need more "exhortation" quickly go on to the next chapter.

Chapter Thirteen

The Three Most Important Words Of A Layman: Attitude, Attitude, Attitude

Zig Zigler the world famous motivational and sales trainer says that attitude not aptitude will determine your altitude. How right he is. Do you feel that you're an optimistic person? Do you always see the glass half full? Do you wake up saying; This day the Lord hath made I shall rejoice and be glad in it. Whatever your answer is you should enjoy this story about the same trip from two different points of view.

It seems there was an optimist and a pessimist on a bicycle built for two. They came upon a big mountain and the optimist said let's "go for it." Let's pedal as hard as we can until we reach the top of the mountain. The pessimist said "no way", we can never make it, that's too difficult. The optimist (who was in the front of the bike) started anyway. Half way up the mountain the optimist was sweating profusely, sweat was just dripping off of him, but he kept on pedaling. Finally, they made it to the top of the mountain where the optimist said to the pessimist, isn't the view beautiful from up here. I told you we could "do it", I told you we could "make it." The pessimist said "yea", but lucky for you I kept the brakes on, or we could have slid right back down.

The above story is amusing, but the moral of the story is so often sad and true. How many of us are going through life with the brakes constantly on. How many of us let negative or scared thoughts of failure prevent us from volunteering our services to the church? How many times have we talked ourselves out of volunteering to help out on a particular project because we let our mind convince us that we just can't do the job? That job is not right for me, we keep telling ourselves. Does this sound familiar?

As an all-star pew-potato this thought ran through my mind constantly. Then I finally figured it out. It all has to do with attitude. So I said to myself, just try one thing, what's the worst that can happen? And I already knew the answer to that, God would turn me into a pillar of Sweet'N Low. I happen to like Sweet'N Low, so it didn't seem so bad to step forward and offer my services.

The most common way to fail is not to start. That means the opposite must be true, that the most common way to succeed in anything is to start. So I am encouraging you here to get started and push yourself to take that first step towards getting **involved** in your church. Have you ever heard this statement before; "it wasn't as bad as I thought it would be." Just about everyone of us has said those words when we stepped out of our comfort zone and tried something different. Our worries are nothing more than misplaced imagination. The only difference in me now as compared to my pew-potato days can be summed up in one word, attitude!

You have a choice to make every morning when you wake up, do you want to be happy, or do you want to be sad? The choice is yours, but remember, the choice you make does effect other people, like your family and friends. Choose to be happy, you will certainly become more popular that way. Plus, if you choose to be happy, your mind will now go to work doing its job of seeking and focusing in on things that bring happiness to you. How do I know your mind will work like this? Because that's the role that God has assigned to your mind, to obey your every command.

Your mind is the most incredible thing God built into you. It will produce back to you all the thoughts that you feed into it. So if you're feeding your mind negative thoughts, your chances of producing great work in any phase of life will be pretty rare. So what happens if you do the opposite and feed your mind nothing but positive thoughts? You'll obviously get the opposite results and your mind will propel you to accomplish great works in all phases of your life. Your mind works just like a computer. Let me give you an illustration of how this process works.

One of the largest computers in the U.S. is in our Space Program (NASA). This computer helps perform all functions on the space shuttle. I think we are all in agreement that it takes a massive and efficient computer to help our astronauts fly the space shuttle into orbit and return safely back to earth. As you can see by the results reported on our TV screens and the media, this computer is doing a splendid job.

But what would happen if we changed the programming of the space shuttle computer? There is computer lingo known as "garbage in - garbage out." What if we programmed the space shuttle computer to think it was a 54 Chevy instead of a highly sophisticated space shuttle. What do you think would happen at lift off? It would probably go to a Drive-In Movie Theatre. A computer is only as good as the information programmed into it. The same process is true of your mind.

The "good news" of this story is that when God created your mind (that computer between your ears), he put in a magnificent highly sophisticated space shuttle capable of handling everything in your life. The "bad news" is that most people think they have a 54 Chevy. Start today, not tomorrow, but today believing that God has equipped you with a space shuttle, and you will begin your journey of discovering the incredible potential that the Lord has placed inside all of His children. They say that potential is God's gift to us, and how we use our potential is our gift back to God. Let's make a vow right here and now to give back to the Lord the greatest gift we can possibly give Him, daily use of our full potential.

When I was 18 years old I had to speak one Sunday morning in our church service. I had just come home from college for Christmas break, and had just finished my first experience with college exams. I was happy to get home away from school and was relieved that the pressure of those exams were now behind me. I was looking forward to partying with my friends when the phone rang. It was the pastor of our church wanting to speak with me. I got nervous, I thought someone was telling him about my weekends at college. It turned out worst than that! He wanted me to speak at church that coming Sunday. I was only 18 at this time and in my mind the pastor was God. There was no way I could say no and not be condemned to hell. At least that's what I thought at the time. So I said that I would speak and he gave me the subject matter he wanted me to talk about. The other college students who were members of the congregation would also be speaking this Sunday. Oh well, there goes my relaxing Christmas break.

Comedians say you should always follow these two golden rules; never let them see you sweat and don't follow someone who is funnier than you are. Well that Sunday that I had to speak in church I spoke after a 22 year old college senior. She was very good. I wasn't. She said some remarkable things that I still remember today. She first told the whole congregation that she was beautiful. This caught my attention in a hurry, because as an 18 year old male with hormones running wild, I felt it was my job to check out members of the opposite sex and determine their beauty. I also felt I did this job extremely well.

Did I consider this speaker to be beautiful? Not at all. I would have called her plain or maybe even used the word homely to describe her. Then after a long pause she finished her sentence. She said she was beautiful in God's eyes. Even as an 18 year old confused college freshman, I knew this girl was right. She was indeed beautiful to the most important person in her life, God. Now that my friends is a positive attitude.

Our beautiful female speaker didn't stop there, she said something that I wish every person in the world could have heard. She said that she has come to realize one remarkable truth about God, and that discovery was this; God doesn't make junk. He never did, and He never will. Amen.

Have you ever realized how important you are to God? Think about this for one moment. There has never been anyone created like you before, and there will never be anyone created like you in the future. That's how unique and special you are to God. That's some awfully powerful and positive proof of God's love for us, wouldn't you agree? So don't let anyone ever tell you that you're average, because they're wrong. Your Creator never made you to be average, so don't you settle for it either. You don't have an average bone in your body. How do I know that you don't have an average bone in your body? Read on...

The number one roadblock to people achieving success in any endeavor in life is self limitation. For some reason our first response to a difficult or new challenge is to say; I can't do that. Unfortunately years of programming have led to that response. That's too bad, because God never put these limitations on you. Instead God filled you with His power, enough power to move a mountain. You don't believe me, then just listen to this power statement; Jesus said, I tell you the truth, if you have faith as small as a mustard seed you can say to this mountain, 'Move from here to there' and it will move (Matt. 17:20 NIV). Wow, now that's power. I'm still learning about this awesome power, and I sure wish that I would have understood about this power back when I was playing high school football. I was a running back, and I think it would have come in handy for me to tell those middle linebackers (they looked like mountains to me) to move from here to there so that I could run by untouched. Why did I have to be such a slow learner?

Let me illustrate in another way the power God has placed inside all of us. I live in New Jersey, and two years ago we had a horrible winter. We had snow storms followed by ice storms it was just incredible. Incredibly bad that is. It was the ice storms that hit us the hardest. You would see these big trees with their branches just bent over hanging down on the road because of all the weight the ice was placing on them. We didn't think spring time would ever come. But guess what, it did. It was amazing. All of the sudden the ice finally started to melt and green buds started to pop up all over the place. Then it dawned on me why this was happening. The strength and the resourcefulness that God had placed in the earth was busting through. It was simply impossible to stop it. Nobody can stop it. Even the government with all its power can't stop it (though they can probably find a way to tax it). This was God displaying His strength. My question to you the reader is this. Why would God not put this same kind of strength and resourcefulness in you, His greatest creation? The answer is simple. HE DID!

So how do you tap into this strength and resourcefulness of God, this must be some kind of ancient mystery, right? Nope. The answer is that you develop an attitude of a giver. Be a giver,

God has always blessed the giver. The Bible is full of stories of people being blessed and every story has one similar or common denominator. The people being blessed were giving a service to others. They were unselfishly helping their fellow man. This is true in both the New Testament and the Old Testament. I'll give you one example from the Old Testament to prove my point.

Abraham did not want his son Issac to marry one of the Canaanite women (Gen. 24). So Abraham sent his servants back to the country he came from in order for them to find the suitable wife for Issac. The servants took 10 of Abraham's camels with them for the journey. The servants decided to go to the well outside the city where the women would come to fill up their water jars every evening. The servants then decided to ask all the women who approached the well for a drink of water, and only the woman who also offers to get water for the camels would be the right one.

Rebekah became this woman, because when the servants asked if she could give them a drink of water, she replied "yes", and told the servants she would also draw water for their camels. You see Rebekah had the attitude of a giver. Because Rebekah had this kind of attitude, it came natural for her to go one step further than the other women and offer to draw water for the camels. And because of Rebekah attitude as a giver, she went on to become one of the most blessed women in the entire Bible.

So if the three most important words in real estate are location, location, and location. Than the three most important words to any layman has got to be attitude, attitude, and attitude.

I read something fascinating the other day by a gentleman named Paul Meyer, who is the founder of Success Motivation Institute in Waco, Texas. Paul made this interesting observation about life that I would like to share with you now. Paul said in his workbook entitled Dynamics Of Personal Goal Setting that we are to picture life as a book with blank pages, and that God has given us the pen to fill this book with whatever we choose. It is now our job to fill these pages with a story of achievement, of personal growth, and of service to mankind that only we have the potential to dream of and make happen.

So how can we possibly make all these great things happen in our lives? Simple, develop the attitude of a giver. Make this kind of attitude happen in your life. Remember Jesus did not come to be served, but to serve (Matt. 20:28). That's the example that Christ set for us. So how about it, why don't you and I try an follow His example. I understand the reward for this is heavenly.

There's a poem about giving that I keep on my desk to remind me everyday of how important it is to have an attitude of a giver. I do not know who wrote this poem nor do I remember who gave it to me. At the time it was given to me I didn't pay much attention to it. I pay attention to it now and I would like to share it with you.

I just simply call this poem "Giving."

> *What! Giving again? I ask in dismay.*
> *And must I keep giving and giving away?*
> *Oh no, said the angel of the Lord looking me through,*
> *Just keep giving till the Master stops giving to you!*

How can I be so positive that God will bless you for being a giver? Well, God has said so himself. Listen to what God says in the Book of Malachi; Bring all the tithes into the storehouse so that there will be food enough in my Temple; if you do, I will open up the windows of heaven for you and pour out a blessing so great you won't have room enough to take it in! (Malachi 3:10 The Living Bible).

During all worship services there will be a segment which is solely dedicated to tithes and offerings. Don't be confused and think that tithes and offerings only deal with money, because it doesn't. Tithes and offerings can also mean gifts or contributions. Our church just like many other churches across the country has special needs that come up from time to time. It's during these special times that sacrificial giving is required. Well some of the people in our congregation are retired and on a fixed income, and giving money at this time would cause real financial hardship to them. But these people still manage to sacrificially give more unto the Lord. What are they giving you might ask? They are giving more of themselves. They donate more of their time and their talents, that is their contribution. They get themselves **involved** in more of the church's activities to help the church reach its spiritual goals.

So lack of money is not an acceptable alibi (I warned you about God's "veto" power). You can have absolutely no money at all and still be a giver, and God has <u>promised</u> that He will overflow the giver with blessings. So much so, that you won't have enough room for them. Having too many blessings from God, I'll take that problem any day of the week. How about you?

I would like to end this chapter with some quotes about attitudes. I ask that you read them and then meditate on what they mean to you.

- If you could kick the person responsible for most of your troubles, you wouldn't be able to sit down for weeks. (This one is my personal favorite. It really hits home for me).
- When life kicks you, let it kick you forward.
- Every miracle in the Bible began with a problem.
- Feed your right attitudes, and before you know it your bad ones will starve to death.
- He who makes no mistakes, makes no progress.
- Fear is nature's warning signal to get busy.
- Well done is better than well said.
- "Be somebody", God didn't take the time to make a nobody.
- The greatest day in your life and mine is when we take total responsibility for our attitudes. That's the day we truly grow up.

Chapter Fourteen

A Pastor's Best Friend
Is Not His Dog

As I mentioned earlier in the book my initial interpretation of a pastor's work week was that they worked one day a week (Sunday), and on this one day they worked a total of 1 to 1 1/2 hours, depending upon how long winded they got during their sermons. The pastors then had the rest of the week off to go play golf, work on their cars, go shopping, or do whatever it is pastors do with their spare time. This sounds like a pretty decent job, doesn't it? If it wasn't for that hating all sins part and doing funerals, I think I would like to apply for this kind of job. I know my golf game would improve if I only had to put in 1 1/2 hours at the old office (church).

The reality of a pastor's work week became known to me when I joined our prayer group that prays for our pastor. Our pastor gave us his weekly schedule, which I naturally assumed would be blank (except for Sunday), and he asked us to pray for the completion of all the items listed on the sheet. Again I thought this sheet would be blank, so I figured it was our prayer group's job to pray that God would put something on this sheet so our pastor would finally have something to do during the week. To my amazement this schedule was full and comprehensive, even during those "off" days of Monday through Saturday, when I thought the church was closed and the pastor was out playing golf. I never imagined our pastor actually had a real job. As a matter of fact his job has more hours in it than mine. Plus he's on 24 hour call every day in case of emergencies. Apparently our pastor needs a beeper, because you never know when a religious emergency might occur. I have now come to this one definite conclusion, I'm sure glad I didn't apply for this job.

What would be some normal activities that your pastor performs during the week? Try these responsibilities on for size:

- Staff Meetings
- Committee Meetings
- Leadership Training
- Administration Duties Of The Church
- Details For Sunday Worship Service
- Long Range Growth Planning For Church
- Short Range Growth Planning For Church
- Congregational Letters & Mailings
- Confirmation Classes
- Special Biblical Teaching Sessions
- On Call 24 Hours For Spiritual Emergencies
- Home Visits
- Shut In Visits
- Hospital Visits
- Sermon Preparation
- Children's Time Material
- Outreach & Follow Up To New Visitors
- New Membership Activity
- Pray For Congregation
- Spiritual Counseling
- Pastor's Hospitality Dinner Parties
- Pastoral Study & Growth Time
- Church & Community Involvement Projects
- Spiritual Reading Time

Take this "normal" week of a pastor and throw in a few holidays, a baptism, a funeral or a wedding and you'll come to the same conclusion I did. Our pastor isn't playing much golf, he doesn't have the time! Wow, when these pastors make a commitment to serve, they really mean it. I wonder if they realize what they're getting into when they're at those fancy religious schools with the crosses on the buildings? If I would have handed this kind of work schedule to our pastor his freshman year in college, I'd bet he'd be selling insurance today.

I hope this illustration makes one point vitally clear to all people attending church. Your pastor can sure use some help in managing this killer of a schedule. The more "little" things the congregation can get involved in, the more relief you will give your pastor. I have to believe that most people genuinely like their pastor. I love our pastor, he's the greatest pastor in the world, and if you're not saying that about your pastor, shame on you. It just makes complete common sense to help someone you like, and your pastor could sure use your help. Any small function of your church's daily activities that you can help out in, pays big dividends to your pastor and your church. Plus the fact it's Biblical to perform these helping functions.

The disciples were constantly doing "little" favors that would eventually pay big and even magnificent dividends to the work of our Lord. A good example of this is found in the Gospel of Mark (Mark 11: 1-11), where the disciples go into a village ahead of Jesus and bring Him back a young colt. This might seem pretty insignificant to you and me, big deal the disciples got Jesus a young colt, so what? Here's where the big dividend comes into play, it would be this young colt that the disciples fetched for Jesus that would carry Him triumphantly into Jerusalem, where all the people would begin to shout; "Hosanna!" "Blessed is he who comes in the name of the Lord"! "Hosanna in the highest!" (Mark 11: 9-10 NIV). You see my friends, it was this "little" favor of fetching the young colt by the disciples that actually started this magnificent event that we refer to today as Palm Sunday.

Another example of this would be Joseph of Arimathea, who had the courage to go to Pontius Pilate and ask for the body of Jesus after the crucifixion. This "small" seemingly innocent part of the Bible is the beginning of the biggest miracle that the world would ever witness, when our God would resurrect His son from the dead. It was during this time that most of the Jewish religious leaders despised Jesus. So it was Joseph of Arimathea "small" leap of courage to give Jesus a proper burial that ended up playing a larger part in God's miraculous plan.

The one individual who I personally feel is the greatest role model, and who possessed the right attitude of a helper that all of us should try to imitate (except for the part of being beheaded) is that of John the Baptist. John the Baptist performed unselfishly in his duties, and his dedicated service definitely helped Jesus' ministry to become as powerful and successful as it was. The Bible teaches us that John the Baptist prepared the way for Christ. The key word in the last sentence is the word prepared. The dictionary gives us this definition for the word prepare; to make ready, usually for a specific purpose. The Bible is obviously instructing us about the importance of preparation (to make ready), and how John the Baptist's preparation was a vital ingredient to the success of the Lord's ministry.

Your church and your pastor have an important ministry to deliver to your local community, and this ministry has got to succeed. Your pastor has the responsibility in his Sunday message to tell the story of what Jesus Christ did on the cross for all us. It's crucial that your pastor be effective in spreading the Gospel and planting seeds of hope in doubters hearts and minds. This is no small task, but it certainly is a worthy task. Let me ask you a question, doesn't a worthy task deserve total preparation? Of course it does. So since we know that's true, it also must be true that your pastor should get the time he needs to prepare to meet this worthy task on a weekly basis.

So how can you and I provide more preparation time and prepare the way for our pastors? Here's how, by chipping in some of our own time and helping out on some of the weekly duties that your pastor is tirelessly performing now. Just imagine what the results would be if everybody in the congregation went up to the pastor and asked him what they could do for him this week? The first thing you'll get is a great big hug from your pastor. The next thing you'll receive is a better church. A church now prepared to burst into greatness that will profoundly effect your entire community. By each member of the congregation sacrificing some of their own time, you'll have now provided the necessary time and opportunity for your pastor to do what he does best, preach the word of God.

This week after the Sunday worship service when you go up to greet your pastor and shake his hand, ask him how you can help? You'll probably get the warmest greeting you've ever received in your life, because that's how pastors get when you give them more time to preach the Gospel of the Lord. Give your pastor that time. You will be preparing the way for your pastor to more effectively reach and win over the people in your community to the Kingdom of God. It's the greatest gift you as a layman can ever give him.

An old adage tells us that a man's best friend is his dog, but that doesn't hold true for pastors (especially our pastor, he owns a cat). A pastor's best friend is you and me. So let's do our best friend, the pastor, a great service and favor this week by lightening up his work load and taking on some of those weekly responsibilities for him. After all, isn't that what best friends in Christ are suppose to do for each other?

Chapter Fifteen

"The Bad News Bible Bears"

God has just placed a classified ad in your local newspaper looking for some new players to join His team. So what would the qualifications be to even get invited to a tryout for God's team? Well, the following is a list of nine famous players (nine symbolizing a baseball team) which I took from the Bible that we'll call God's all-star team, and let's examine briefly their credentials.

Here's the starting line up and vital statistics for the Bible all-star team:

1. Abraham — Considered the founder of the Jewish nation, and his faithfulness impressed God immensely. He was also a liar. Twice in the Book of Genesis Abraham lied about his wife Sarah and told people she was his sister so no harm would come to him. Apparently the husband being the protector for his family was not a popular theory during the time of Abraham.

2. Issac — The famous son of Abraham and Sarah. Like father, like son, Issac also was a liar. According to the Book of Genesis he too lied about his wife Rebekah and said she was his sister so that no harm would come to him.

3. Peter — A disciple of Jesus, known as the rock. Peter was also a big fat liar documented by all four of the Gospel writers. Obviously this rock crumpled quite a bit. He swore he would die for Christ and then went out and denied him not once, but three times in order to save his own skin. Peter would later redeem himself, and become one of the leading voices in building the first churches.

4. David — Considered the most famous King of Israel. Jesus would be a descendant of this royal line. David not only committed adultery with Bathsheba, but he also plotted the murder of her

husband Uriah to try and cover up his mistake. King David had about as much success in covering up his mistakes as President Nixon did with Watergate.

5. Noah — Survived God's great flood by building an ark. The Book of Genesis tells us that Noah was a righteous man. Noah was also a drunk and an exhibitionist (Genesis 9: 21-25). Noah got drunk and embarrassed himself in front of his sons by his nakedness. His son's were so embarrassed that they took some cloth and walked into Noah's tent backwards in order to cover up their father's nakedness.

6. John The Baptist — He prepared the way for our Lord. John the Baptist would have to be considered a homeless person by our standards today (he lived in the wilderness). And he was also a convict who spent some time in prison.

7. Paul — Could be considered the greatest apostle in the entire Bible. Paul first became famous by persecuting every Christian that came in his path, and was seen cheering loudly while Stephen was being stoned to death (Acts 8:1). Paul was also a convict who spent considerable time in prison. As a matter of fact, Paul was lucky that the Crime Bill with the "Three Strikes And Your Out" provision wasn't in play during his time period. This provision definitely would have crippled Paul's activities during his ministry.

8. Lot — The Bible tells us that God saved Lot from the destruction of Sodom and Gomorrah. Lot would also have to be considered the first potential child abuser (Genesis 19:8). Lot in order to save and protect his two male visitors from an angry mob of men from Sodem, offers them his two daughters for the angry men to do what they like with them. I'm sure every woman and mother in the world will have a chosen word or two to say to Lot when God calls them home to heaven.

9. Thomas — One of the twelve disciples chosen by our Lord Jesus, who developed a self inflected problem (doubt) due to a lack of faith. Thomas didn't buy into any part of the resurrection story that his friends were telling him about. He doubted it actually happened and refused to believe it until he personally saw with his own eyes the nail prints in our Lord's hands.

I look at the qualifications of these all-stars and I have to say that God's team resembles "The Bad News Bears" or make that "The Bad News Bible Bears." I now understand why the prison fellowship ministry is so critically important to God. It seems that a lot of His best players started their careers from behind bars. I'm pretty sure even I can measure up to these fellow's qualifications. As I mentioned earlier in this book, I lied to my secular friends about going to Bible Study in the beginning. So apparently I'm on the right track and have a bright future to making God's "dream team."

Why would God want all these social misfits on His team? What does all of this have to say about the make-up of God's glorious team? It tells me that <u>everybody</u> qualifies to be on it. Apparently God doesn't cut anyone from His team. He can take a person possessing terrible characteristics and still perform magnificent accomplishments through them. God has consistently shown that He will accept people from every level of society and use them for His good. Our Lord seems to specialize in recognizing our human weakness, and then turning that same weakness into a strength for His team.

I recently read that most people feel they don't deserve God's love and forgiveness because of some of the awful things they have done in the past. Well take a good hard look at some of these famous Bible people on God's all-star team, and look at their past history. I'm starting to feel like a saint compared to what some of these folks have done. Yet God forgave them all completely, and then used them to accomplish spectacular feats for His Kingdom here on earth. This is certainly encouraging news to both you and I, wouldn't you agree?

So what is God looking for in people so that they can effectively play on His team? God is looking for people who will take action. He doesn't need anymore bench sitters, there's too many of them on the team already. He needs active players on his team, people who are willing to attempt things for God based upon faith alone. That's what kind of players God needs on His team right now.

My closest friend at church, a gentleman by the name of Rick

Shoyer, gave me a great illustration of this precise point. He asked me who was the MVP in the Major League's last year (1994)? I said "nobody", the season was canceled because of the strike. My friend then asked, but why wasn't there an MVP for the season? I said because they didn't play the games last year. He said correct, and the same principle applies to God's team. You can't expect to be an MVP on God's team if you don't play in the game. And playing in God's game is simply getting yourself **involved** in your church's efforts to spread God's word in your local community. Just showing up at the stadium (the church) is not enough, you have to run out onto the playing field and start playing.

I have tried most of my life to be a bench sitter, but God wouldn't let me. God refused to let me get comfortable on the bench and maybe that's what's happening in your life at this moment. You're starting to squirm a little bit in your pew seat. You feel kind of funny about avoiding some of your church's activities. It's at this point where God is speaking directly to your heart. That's exactly how it started with me. God stopped me from burying my face in the Hymnals every time someone would ask for volunteers to help out at the church. Then God finally nudged me onto the playing field.

Did I feel strange being a member on God's team? A little bit in the beginning, as I have already stated earlier in the book. But then I remembered who my teammates were, people like Abraham, Issac, King David, and Paul. And I remembered that they were all great sinners just like me. So you see, there is nothing to be nervous about, is there? I figure if Paul "the convict" can make God's all-star team, why can't I? And the answer is I can, if I'm willing to apply myself to His work.

Almighty God has consistently displayed that He doesn't prejudge His players by their past failures and sins. Praise the Lord for this, because if He did <u>nobody</u> could ever make His team. God sent His only Son to the cross to take care of our failures and sins, so now because of Christ, we have the glorious opportunity to be placed on God's opening day roster. We must get ourselves prepared to play, I understand it's a long season, and there are no "home games" on this schedule since our real home is heaven. So let's "play ball", it's time for us to take the field, that's the one qualification that guarantees <u>all</u> of us a spot on God's all-star team.

Chapter Sixteen

Conclusion: "The Peeling Of The Potato"

I was asked this week if I would be part of our church mowing team. I'll have to admit that my old pew-potato thoughts came rushing back to me. I mean what's this mowing team all about? Why are we mowing our own lawn? Why can't the church find some "Jesus Freak" Landscaper who will cut the church lawn for free because he is doing it for Christ, and can get a nice tax break for his business at the same time? Think about that for a minute. I think I have created a win-win situation. The "Jesus Freak" Landscaper gets blessings from God for mowing the church lawn, and gets a tax break for his business. What a great concept. How come nobody in the church ever thinks of these great ideas? I guess it takes a professional pew-potato to move the church into the "real" world of wheeling and dealing.

It turns out that God had laid on the hearts of our church leadership group that the "Jesus Freak" Landscaper was not a good idea for our church. Boy, I wish I was there when they took this vote. It must have been a secret vote because I don't recall seeing anything about this in our church bulletin. Apparently our church members have been mowing the church lawn for over 125 years, and that's the way it will continue until God tells our church leadership group something different. So if God has been pleased with the way our members have cut the church lawn for all these years, I guess I better start keeping my ideas to myself. I don't want to get the Big Guy mad at me.

I prayed about this decision (see I'm getting better), and then said "yes" to the mowing team. Once again I am validating my expensive four year college degree in business. Let's face it, those

Lawn Boy mowers can get tricky, and it takes a college fellow like me to handle the crisis of figuring out where the gas and oil goes in.

I understand that if I can pass the church lawn mowing test, that I will have the opportunity to be upgraded to weed-wacker patrol. The only problem I can foresee me having with the weed-wacker is that by church rules you can only use the weed-wacker outside the building. What a shame. I definitely don't agree with this policy. I think the weed-wacker would be fantastic for using between the pews after church service to clear out all the stuff the kids have dropped. Trust me, I'm already on the cleaning team and they haven't invented the vacuum cleaner that can pick up some of the stuff kids drop on any given Sunday. Just ask any parent they'll verify this point. So come on church leadership group, loosen up, let me inside with my weed-wacker. You'll be thanking me later. Just you wait and see.

I'm glad to be a part of our mowing team and I only have to mow the church lawn once the whole summer. Why only one time you might ask? Because lots of other people are **involved** in this project with me. That's my main focus on everything I have written so far. That if you get **involved** with just mowing the lawn like I did, you will make it easier on everybody else who has volunteered for this same project. This kind of cooperation from the members certainly makes your church run more smoothly. There is nothing worst than the church burning out their good workers. I always thought that over worked lay people was the pastor's problem not mine. Wrong! It's the whole congregation's problem, because it's the lack of congregational **involvement** that caused this problem in the first place. And the only person in the church who can fix this problem is the same person you see every time you look into a mirror. That's right, it's you. Not the pastor, but you. Each individual has to take personal responsibility for their commitment to the church. This was the hardest lesson for me to learn.

You see I wanted to have it both ways. I wanted to have Christ in my life, but I also wanted to have no **involvement**. It sounded like a good plan to me, I even made a promise to myself to be an extra nice person to make up for my lack of **involvement**. God loves extra nice people, doesn't He? Well apparently God loves all people, not just extra nice people, so He did not allow me to get away with this type of strategy. Once again God placed His "veto" on my plans. I have since found out you cannot override God's "veto" power. Luckily for me I learned this lesson faster than Jonah, or I would now be dictating my thoughts from inside Shamu the Killer Whale.

At this point I'm hoping some of you are asking why did I, an ordinary layman, decide to write this book? Well I'm glad you finally asked. It's because people and their behavior have always fascinated me. Let me use shopping at the Mall as my example. When my wife takes me to the Mall shopping, I go kicking and screaming every time. I really do hate shopping. I don't know why, but I just hate it. It must be a guy thing. Maybe this was God's real punishment to women when Eve took a bite out of that apple. Think about it for a moment. Some women could escape God's wrath by deciding not to have children and totally avoid that child pain thing. God had to shut down this loop hole in his plan. So what God really said to Eve after she bite the forbidden apple, was that your punishment will be to bear pain during child birth and to have your husband be a great big royal pain in your butt every time you take him shopping. God had now covered all of the angles.

When I am forced to go shopping, I ask my wife for one favor. She can shop as long as she wants (one hour tops), if I can just hang out in the middle of the Mall and check people out. I have a great wife and she always grants this small favor. I like to check out couples and try to figure out how they met. Sometimes I will see a beautiful woman with a not so good looking man. What is my initial reaction to this? The guy must have money. What else could she see in him. Be honest now, we all have made observations like this when we see two people who in our judgment don't seem to be a match.

What does all of this have to do with this book? Everything. I was observing the different committee's in our church and I noticed one common element about the people on them. The same people were on all of the committees. I realized this when I became Committee Chairperson for the Capital Stewardship Committee (the committee that gets to use the nice church stationery). I was just getting ready to launch my complaint about the lack of **involvement** from the congregation when I took a good hard look at myself and realized that for 99% of my church life, I was on the other side of the fence of not being **involved**. I figured what right did I have to reprimand people for not getting **involved** with their church when I had spent most of my life dodging this same issue. I didn't want to be a hypocrite, at least not this week, it wasn't my turn. Besides the church has enough hypocrites, right people?

So now you are reading the answer that I felt God led me to. I've decided to take this "popular" subject of getting **involved** with your church activities to the public. I believe God chose me to write this book because I'm no different than you the reader. I have no theology training whatsoever, and that's probably good for this message. Am I the best layman in my church? No, not even close. Am I the most active laymen in my church? Again no, not even close. As a matter of fact, it was only five years ago when I wasn't even attending church services at all. Are there more qualified people than me to be writing about this subject matter? Absolutely, scores of them. Have I ever written a book before? No, I have never even thought about it before. But for some strange reason God has placed it on my heart to write this book. You would think that some well known Christian author would be explaining to all layman the importance of your work in the church. Well, wouldn't you? I guess God had other ideas. Apparently He wanted you to read it from another layman's point of view. I told you God works in reverse of most of our human plans.

So what kind of success will this book have coming from an unknown layman author? Only God knows for sure. If this book sells a million copies, I think that would be great. If you are the only one who ever reads this book, I think that's great also. I'm putting this in God's hands, and will let Him place it in the hands of those that He feels it can benefit. So I am grateful that the Lord has chosen you to be one of the readers. I hope this book gives you a few laughs and a lot to think about on how your **involvement** can help your church become a better church than it is today. Believe it or not, you are the key ingredient to your church's overall success.

God has successfully peeled the skin off of this all star pew-potato. The best way I can describe this journey for me is that it's like an amusement park ride that never ends, and you don't want it to end. The ride started out slowly (the cleaning team) which I appreciated at that time, but it keeps on accelerating as I keep growing in service to Him.

What happens to a child when you place them on their favorite ride? What will they always yell once the ride begins? Make it go faster, make it go faster, right! Well the same exact experience is now happening in this former pew-potato's life. I have taken on the enthusiasm of a child, and I'm yelling at the owner of the amusement park (God) to make my ride (my **involvement**) go faster. You can learn a lot about God by watching the actions of a child. It certainly has helped me grow in my understanding of the Lord. And it provided me with this neat analogy of the amusement park rides. Thanks Kids.

So do I think that the Lord will let me stay on this ride forever? Absolutely! How do I know this to be true? God told me through His son Jesus. He specifically told me that I could stay on this ride until Jesus comes back to get me. If you need more proof, read for yourself; And be sure of this - that I am with you always, even to the end of the world (Matt. 28:20 The Living Bible). I told you that I had permission to stay on this ride.

My only regret about this magnificent ride is that not enough people are on it. I understand that God will make this ride even more spectacular if some more people will hop on. So help me out won't you? It seems that for me to get more enjoyment out of this ride I need your help. I need you to join me on this wonderful ride that God has placed me on. How can you help me experience a greater thrill on this ride? It's simple. Get **involved** with your church's activities. Volunteer to help out the next time a project comes up in your church. Then Almighty God will place you on this wonderful ride with me. I look forward to meeting you.

So what's the big rush to get **involved** with your church today? It's because exciting times lie ahead for all churches. Churches are going to explode with activity in the 90's and into the next century. Look at the political atmosphere right now. Everybody is reporting that our country is making a giant shift to the right. People are beginning to realize what the core problem is in our country. The problem is decaying morals. I firmly believe this country is now prepared to declare war against this problem and change the direction we are now heading in.

Our nation has come to the conclusion that we don't need any more expensive government programs to cover up our existing problems. We need to correct our country's value system and the church (including your hometown church) is going to lead the way. Now that's excitement!

I saw an article in the newspaper today talking about crimes committed by children. The question the reporter asked was when did this start to occur in our society and how do you stop it? I'm sure this reporter thought that he had asked a tough question with no answer to be found. But he's wrong. The answer has always been there staring us right in the face.

When did crimes committed by children start becoming rampant in our society? The day after the Supreme Court took God out of the school systems, that's when. So what's our solution to stopping this growing problem in our country? REVERSE THE ACTION. Put God back into our schools. Start teaching our children the Ten Commandments. That wasn't so difficult, was it? This answer makes a lot of sense so it's a safe bet that no politician will come up with it. And this answer doesn't cost the tax payer a penny.

The popular slogan that's going around now is "Dan Qualye Was Right", referring to his family values speech that drew sharp criticism from the liberal media. Of course Dan Qualye was right, anybody speaking about family values is right. It's keeping the family unit together that will solve our welfare system permanently, not some big government welfare reform program. Jesus said; the spirit of the Lord is upon me, because he hath annointed me to preach the Gospel to the poor (Luke 4:18 KJV). Jesus knew that the poor people didn't need government support to get out of their situation, they needed to hear the word of Almighty God. And who plays a vital role in spreading the word of God about moral values and about keeping the family unit together? You got it, your local neighborhood church. That's their job.

So as you can see the church is going to have a major role in the coming years, and they need our help to meet this responsibility. My church, your church, all the churches in this nation are going to pull together and change the direction this country is headed in.

The future of our country looks very bright to me. Because of the expanded **involvement** of the church in our society our children will now be taught moral values and respect both at home and in the schools. When this finally occurs (and it will) you can rest assured we will stop reading in our newspapers about children committing crimes. You see a child who truly knows God is not capable of committing such acts.

So come on, you can do it. I know you can. The time is right now for you to get off of the sidelines and into the game. It's now your golden opportunity to pick up the ball and run, and run with it for God's glory. That's why God had me write this book, because if I, the former all-star pew-potato can do it, so can you.

A gentleman by the name of Larry Eisenberg said it best when he stated that the smallest deed is better than the grandest intention. How right he was. My smallest deed started with cleaning the church bathroom, and now look what God's doing with me. He has me writing a book. Can He do the same thing for you? Absolutely! But you must take that first step. So there's only one question that still remains. What's going to be your smallest deed?

Let me finish with one little suggestion from one layman to another. As a matter of fact this last suggestion I'm going to make will only take me two words. Here it is: **GET INVOLVED.**

- **"The harvest is plentiful but the workers are few. Ask the Lord of the harvest, therefore, to send out workers into his harvest field." (Matt. 9:37-38 NIV)**

What Can A Church Do For You?

On Thursday evening August 31, 1995, the lives of Tracie and Greg Gregoris were about to be changed. That night we received a phone call from Tracie's OB/GYN doctor urging us to set an appointment with a physician that he referred to as an oncologist. My wife and I had no clue what an oncologist was so we pressed the doctor for a more clear answer. He said he received some unusual results from a blood test that he ran, he called this test a CA125, and he wanted another physician (the oncologist) to check it out. This answer was not good enough for us so we pressed even harder for an explanation. We wanted the doctor to tell us specifically why he wanted us to waste our valuable time setting up an appointment with another doctor. Finally the doctor came clean and told us in one sentence the most horrifying news that either of us had ever heard in our entire lives. He said, "Tracie, I think you have cancer."

We were able to set an appointment with the oncologist for Tuesday, September 5th. Those were the longest four days of our lives. After my wife's examination on Tuesday our new doctor said that there is no way to be sure the tumor she had on her ovary was cancerous. The only way to know for sure would be through surgery and to remove the tumor. They did an MRI, an ultrasound and another CA125 test, but unfortunately for us the results of this test were worse than the first one. Surgery was now set up for Monday morning October 16th.

It was now time to tell our families, friends and church what was about to happen in our lives. I knew our families and friends would give us total support, that was a given. Both my wife and I are blessed with wonderful families. But it was our church family's response to our crisis that kind of caught us off guard. As I mentioned earlier in the book Tracie and I attend Bunker Hill Presbyterian Church. This church with about 200 members in all took it upon themselves to declare "war" against the tumor that had invaded my wife's body. They united as Christian soldiers to help fight this illness that had attacked my wife. What weapons did God arm these Christian soldiers with? The most powerful weapon our history books have ever taught us about. God armed these soldiers from Bunker Hill Presbyterian Church with the power of prayer.

Everybody, and I do mean everybody, in our church was praying to God to lay His healing touch upon Tracie. One night our Bible Study group laid hands on my wife while we prayed for God to heal her. It's impossible for me to put in words how emotional and powerful that prayer was. It literally brought my wife and me to tears.

Finally October 16th came, the day of surgery to remove the tumor was upon us. For some reason I was extremely calm that day. They took my wife to get her ready for the surgery and then called for me to see her one more time before they wheeled her into the operating room. At this moment I lost my calmness. I saw my wife, the person I love more than anything on this earth, about to go through the most frightening experience in her life. I wanted to push her off the hospital gurney and get on it myself and tell the doctor to operate on me not my wife. I wanted this tumor to be in my body, not hers. I remember giving my wife two kisses and telling her that I loved her. The hospital assistant then wheeled her away to the operating room with tears in her eyes. Another assistant took me tearfully away to another room called the surgical waiting room. The surgical waiting room was on the other side of the hospital and the walk to get there seemed like a week to me. I was a wreck and I felt so helpless. I just wanted to cry like a baby but I kept telling myself I had to be strong. The only thing that was keeping me going at this moment was the powerful reminder that Tracie was in God's hands.

At 8:20 a.m. while I was in the surgical waiting room a hospital assistant came up to me and told me the surgery had just begun. I bowed my head and prayed for the doctor and his surgical team that God would work through them. At 10:30 a.m. the hospital assistant told me our doctor was on the phone from the operating room and he wanted to speak with me. The assistant led me to a private room with a telephone where our doctor stated the following: "Greg, I removed the tumor from Tracie and it was benign." That was the greatest phone call I have ever received in my life. Our doctor then informed me he was going to repair my wife's damaged fallopian tube, something that was not even a part of the operation. But isn't that how God always works, to give His people a little extra. When God answers prayers He always seems to bless you with more than you expected. For some unknown reason God had decided to put us on the "bonus plan." Wait just a minute, this reason was not unknown. God was simply answering all the prayers that were lifted up to Him by our family, friends and church.

When the doctor told me on the phone the good news about my wife's surgery and that he was going to repair her fallopian tube I told the doctor that our Bible Study group was praying specifically for him during this operation. Here is how the doctor responded to my comment: "This operation went very smooth, obviously God was listening to your people." I responded: "He always does, that's His promise."

I realize and understand that my family is not the only family to have the threat of cancer enter into their lives. But I don't understand how any family can cope with this crisis situation without faith. God was the only thing my wife and I had to hold onto during this entire episode. Just knowing that so many other people were petitioning God on our behalf to heal Tracie was very comforting and brought great relief during this turbulent time. I now comprehend why it is so important to be a witness for Christ in my life. I need to share with more people about what Christ did in my life so that they can have hope and believe that our Lord is in total control even during times of trials and suffering. A good question to ask right now is where did my wife and I get this hope and belief system from that carried us through our crises? Here's the answer: Our Church!

Am I saying that our church actually had something to do with the successful outcome of Tracie's surgery? You bet I am! There is absolutely no doubt in my mind that God heard all the prayers lifted up for Tracie. But God didn't stop there, no not our God. Our God is a God of action, so He decided to give us a reply to our prayers. And I am so very grateful to His reply because God said "yes" to our prayers and went ahead and healed her.

I want to take this time to apologize for not applying any humor to this chapter. But during this difficult time in my life there were not a lot of funny thoughts running through my mind. I would like to finish this chapter by going back to the very beginning of the chapter and pose the question of what can a church do for you? My answer for you the reader to mediate upon and share with others is this: It will save your life in more ways than you could ever possibly imagine, both here on earth and in heaven.

P.S. - I look forward to seeing you at church next Sunday. And May God Bless.

REFERENCES

"When God Whispers Your Name", By Max Lucado, Word Publishing.

"Dynamics of Personal Goal Setting", by Paul J. Meyer. Success Motivation Institute, Inc., Waco, Texas.

"See You At The Top", by Zig Zigler. The Zig Zigler Corp., Carrollton, Texas.

"Unwrap Your Spiritual Gifts", by John C. Maxwell and Dan M. Reiland. Skyline Wesleyan Church, Lemon Grove, CA.

Ron Blue, Managing Partner of Ron Blue & Co., Atlanta, Georgia. "Storm Shelter", Thomas Nelson Publications, a Janet Thoma Book, Copyright 1994 by Ron Blue.

Achievement Dynamics Institute, by Mario Pinardo, Cherry Hill, NJ.